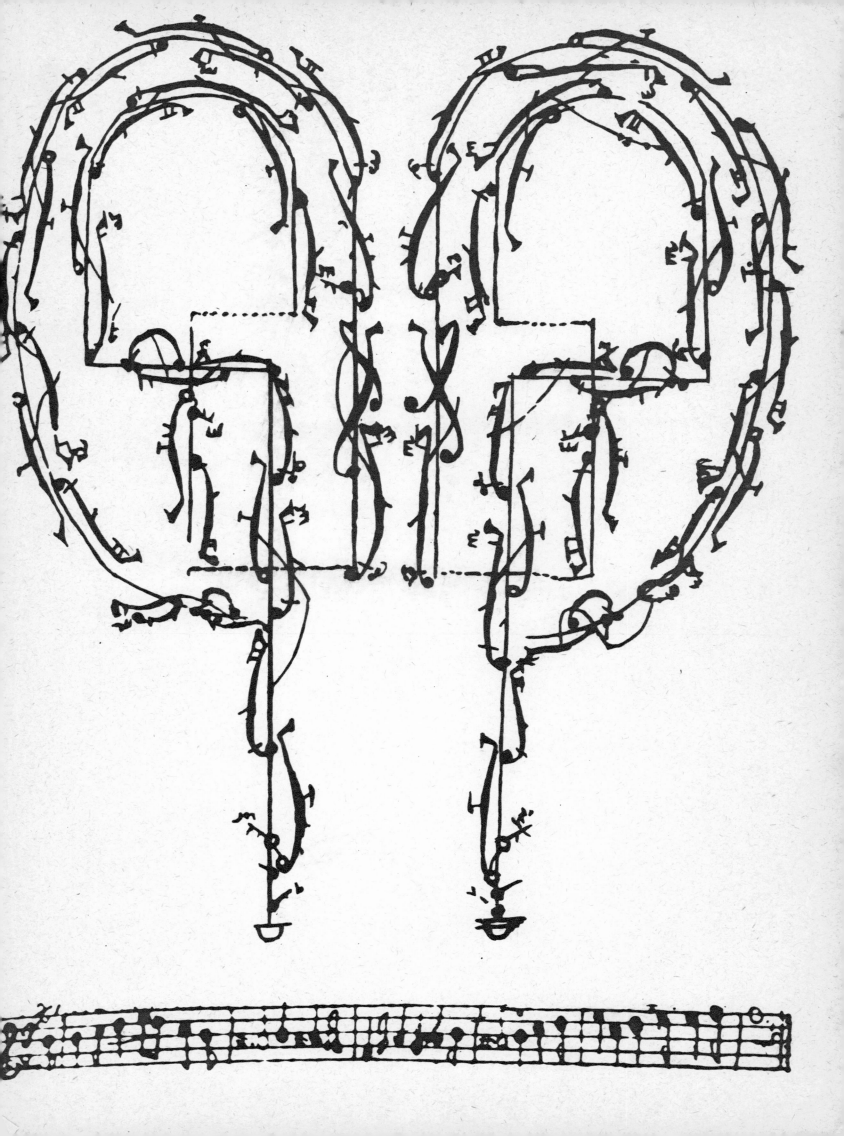

Contents

Designer   Germano Facetti
Editor   David Lambert
Art   Patricia Lockie
   Bruce Robertson
   Perez Roman
   Peter Sullivan

Printed in Great Britain by L.T.A. Robinson Ltd. London

Arnold L. Haskell

The Wonderful World of
Dance

Garden City Books
Garden City New York

© 1960 Rathbone Books Limited

A sequence of still photos of a moving body (left), a sketch of strips fixed to moving leg and arm (right) reveal rhythm underlies all human movements; an athlete's and a ballerina's leap.

What is Dance?

This book is about dancing: dancing all over the world from Stone Age man to the ballet dancer Margot Fonteyn. It is an important and a vast subject; there are no peoples who are without their dances, whether we are thinking of boomerang-throwing natives in Australia or modern city dwellers with their rock 'n' roll. The way in which people dance and their reasons for dancing tell us a great deal about their way of living and thinking. Similarly the records which reveal how past peoples lived and thought help us to recreate a number of the ways in which they danced.

What we know about dancing through the ages is largely guesswork, guesses arrived at from several clues: from what we know about primitive tribes living today, from ancient drawings and carvings, but mostly from what we know of ourselves and our feelings. Most human feelings are instincts common both to statesmen and the simple-minded, to 20th century man and men living 20,000 years ago.

We believe that dancing is an instinct. In other words something within each of us *makes* us want to dance. We "dance with joy" if anyone brings us good news, or we "dance with pain" if we bang our thumb with a hammer. In a foreign country we wave our hands and arms in an attempt to make people understand us. In Italy, the people gesticulate naturally and gracefully in everyday conversations with one another. It is surprising how many ideas can be expressed in this way.

Although these instinctive movements tell us something about dancing, they are not the kind of dancing this book is about. The broad question to which we shall attempt to give an answer in the following pages is *what is dancing?*

The words "dance" and "dancing" come from an old German word *danson* which means "to stretch." All dancing is made up of stretching and relaxing. The muscles are tensed for leaping and then relaxed as we make what we hope will be a gentle and graceful landing. But clearly dancing must be something organized and not merely jumping around in a state of temper, hunger or excitement. A good answer to the question would be to say that dancing is expressing one's emotions through movement disciplined by rhythm.

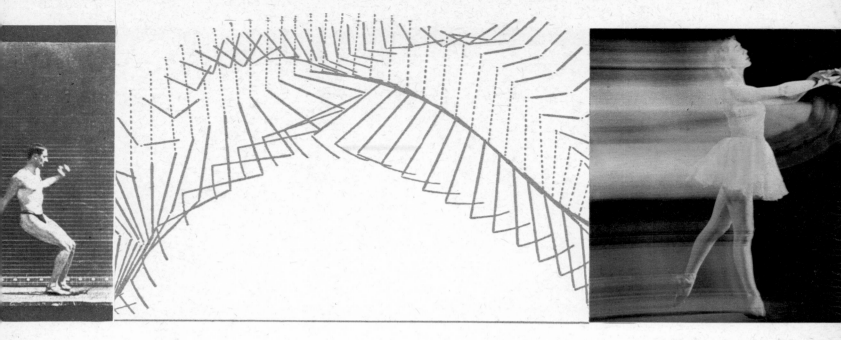

631919

Everyday rhythmic movements help human bodies overcome obstacles but dance movements discipline rhythm to reveal human feelings.

How did dancing begin? Why should movements be rhythmical? The answer can be found in the universe around us and in ourselves.

Before any living thing existed on earth, the universe of galaxies, stars, planets, moons was a great rhythmic creation moving through space: planets circling their suns, moons circling their planets. On our planet, earth, the movement of the earth around the sun, and the moon around the earth, created the rhythms of day and night, of the tides. Later, when living plants appeared, winter and summer created rhythms of growth and decay. On this world evolved ever changing species of creatures, themselves kept alive by the rhythmic beating of their hearts, the rhythmic breathing of their lungs, the rhythmic swimming, running or flying of their bodies.

Long before man appeared, many of these animals deliberately danced, as apes, birds and other creatures still dance. Their dance was prompted by the rhythms of life which pulsed through their bodies and through the universe.

Above: The universe is built on rhythm, from the rhythmic motion of the planets to the rhythmic pattern of this prehistoric shell. Below: The urge to dance is in us from our childhood when life's rhythms pulsing through our bodies are our only dancing teachers.

Rhythmic patterns underlie all art, from a masterpiece by Michelangelo to this Indian fabric from Peru. Its five different-colored threads are interwoven to produce three patterns. The repetition of these color patterns builds up a rhythm to create a work of art.

Man's first dances probably began in the same way. Many dances of primitive tribes still living are said to be identical with those of birds and apes.

Human dancing, therefore, is as old as the first man who expressed his feelings of joy or fear by rhythmically repeated steps or leaps or gestures, perhaps 25,000 years ago. Dancing may well be the oldest of all the arts, an art that needs no instrument, not even a twig or a piece of rock. The instrument is the dancer's body. Music came later. The "music" of early man came from stamping feet and clapping hands that supplied the rhythm for the dance.

Dance, music, all arts depend on rhythm, as the earliest artists realized. We can see this in the rhythmic pattern of a bushman's woven basket, in the rhythmic repetition of phrases in a native poem or story, the rhythmically repeated notes of a primitive song. We see rhythm most clearly in the dance – the art of movement – whether in the simple leap of the savage or the sophisticated *pirouette* of the ballet dancer. Rhythms flow through all the arts in all ways of life.

This simple native work song depends on repeated rhythmic words as much as the most complex mass. All music, poetry, painting, dancing, is built on patterns of notes, words, shapes or steps.

Aw, ha ya ha ya ha
ha ya he ya a
he ya ha ya a
A, ha ya ha ya ha
aw, ha ya he ya ha
he ya ha ya hei
ya ha
ha ha wo wo wo.

Aw, ha ya ha ya ha
ha ya he ya a
he ya ha ya a
A, ha ya ha ya ha
aw, ha ya he ya ha
he ya ha ya hei
ya ha
ha ha wo wo wo.

9

This running chain dance needs a great deal of space for its performance. It flourishes on the flat expanse of Russia's steppes.

Dancing is world-wide, but throughout the world dances differ. In one land only men dance, in another, only women. Elsewhere, men and women dance together in couples. The dance may be quick or slow, gay or solemn. How have so many dances grown up in different parts of the world?

The answer lies partly in the dancers' environment: the natural surroundings in which they live. Compare the life of a dweller in a mountain village with the life of a farmer in the valley below. The mountain dweller lives perhaps among hills too steep, too rugged, too stony to grow crops; yet hills which support sheep, goats or cattle nimble-footed enough to scramble for scattered tufts of grass among the rocks. To survive here the hillman must be a hunter or herdsman, walking many miles a day over the roughest country, his eyes raised to the hill slopes ahead. He develops an alert, springing step, walks with his weight on his toes.

The plainsman lives often on a flat expanse of rich soil where crops grow abundantly. His whole life may be devoted to tending the same few fertile acres, his eyes cast down to the earth beneath his feet as he ploughs, sows, harrows or reaps. The plainsman develops a slow, heavy tread, walks with

Leaping dances display the fine physique of these natives, adapted to the tropics where tall slim bodies swiftly lose excess heat.

Europe's leaping dances require little level space. They flourish equally on Macedonian mountainsides and the North German Plain.

his weight on his whole foot. Their environments affect not only the way these people gain a living, but the very way they walk.

Their everyday movements are enough to suggest that hill dances would be more lively than plains dances. Natural environment makes them even more different: with little level space to dance on, the hillman may develop only springing, leaping steps. On the broad village greens of the valley below, plainsmen have space for running dances, taking up a great deal of level ground.

Thus in the Bavarian mountains of southern Germany a popular folk dance was the *ländler*, in which men would throw their girl partners high in the air. On the level Russian steppes, dancers form a chain needing a large, flat space for its pattern of horizontal movements.

Here we have simply suggested how mountains and valleys help to produce different dances. Throughout the world great differences in rainfall and temperature produce tropical and arctic regions, swamps and deserts. In almost every region man has gained a foothold. Unconsciously he adapts himself, his way of life and his dances to the particular environment in which he lives.

Arctic climates encourage Eskimos to put on heat-conserving body fat. Physique and furry clothes affect the way these people dance.

To Salampasu tribesmen in Central Africa, dancing remains a magic act, to "bring about" events which muscle-power cannot achieve.

To wealthy Indian rajahs, two centuries ago, dancing meant only entertainment. Expert performers amused them and their guests.

Dancing in different lands actually differs less than dancing for different reasons. Dancing probably began as we have suggested, as a rhythmic expression of happiness, but it was rapidly put to "practical" use.

If rains failed and fleet-footed animals fled to distant pastures, man the hunter might starve. If wild pigs broke into his grain fields and ate the unripe harvest, man the farmer might starve. Like his animal prey and pests, early man was at the mercy of nature. Unlike the beasts, he knew it.

What he could not make happen with his muscles alone, he tried to effect with his mind. He imitated in a dance what he wanted to happen. Before a hunt he mimed a hunt, including the killing of his prey. Many early magical dances probably began as pantomime rituals. The steps he danced were important to man not because they were beautiful but because they *meant* something. They must always be repeated in the same way for the spell to work.

But with the world's first civilizations, man's way of life changed. Better food production, more specialized manufacturers and merchants supported a leisured class of priests, nobles and a king. With time, power and money at his disposal, the king wanted entertainment. Dancing girls performed before him, inventing new, spectacular dances: acrobatic leaps and handstands – all to please their royal patron. The steps they danced were not important because they had meaning, like those of magical dances in a primitive tribe, but because they were more graceful or skilful than those which ordinary people could perform.

Today we still find magical dances in lands where man does not benefit from modern discoveries in science and machinery, where he is unable to control nature's pests and plagues. We find spectacular dancing in lands where mechanization has produced a class of people with plenty of leisure time and money to spend on the enjoyment of watching experts paid to dance.

In almost all ages and all lands we find the dance for pleasure – the social dance – the most enjoyably active way devised for meeting an old friend or making the acquaintance of a future wife. Most people are gregarious: they like to live in communities rather than alone. Thus the social dance plays its part in palace as well as village square, is danced by the rich as well as the poor, by the savage and the city businessman.

People dance for joy in every land and age: in Flanders, pictured here 400 years ago; from Singapore to Santiago at the present day.

Labyrinth patterns on ancient Greek coins hint at the forgotten ritual steps which underlie the farandole, *still danced in France today.*

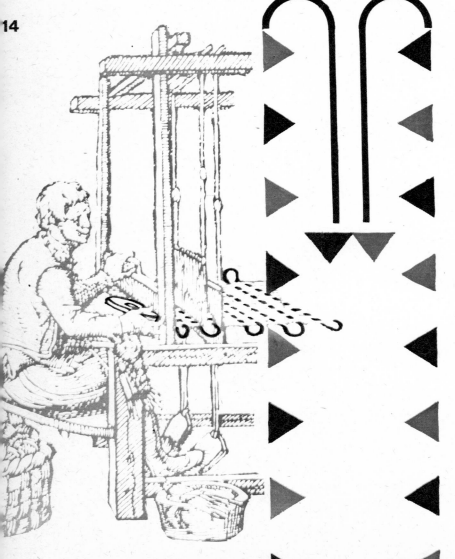

Dance steps grow out of time and place, ever changing as man shapes environment to change his way of life. The steps we dance today are quite unlike the way we run to catch a bus to work. But could we trace their pattern through the past we should most likely find that once they formed the movements of a magic rite, itself a vital part of everyday life.

We can trace few dances in this way. The clues are scattered. Often they seem unrelated to the dance. Who would connect the labyrinth of ancient Crete, the children's game of hopscotch and the *farandole* still performed in southern France?

The snake-like windings of the *farandole* of Provence – an ancient colony of Greece – closely resemble a journey to the middle of a labyrinth depicted on an ancient Greek coin. The labyrinth pattern once stood for the passage of a dead man to heaven, a passage fraught with danger from threatening evil powers. People who performed a funeral dance to the middle of a man-made laby-rinth believed they helped the dead man on his way.

Its reason long forgotten, this ancient dance survives both in the "snail shell" into which the leader winds the dancers of a *farandole* and,

In Sweden's "Weaving Dance" a man and woman run between two lines of facing couples in imitation of a shuttle thrown across a loom.

Hops on numbered squares towards a "paradise," or goal, suggest that hopscotch, like other dancing games, was once a magic rite.

indirectly, in the hops on numbered squares of hopscotch – a children's dance game with a goal.

The history of hopscotch is uncertain: some think it started as a Christian rite. Probably it was already old by the time Christ was born, for early Christians borrowed pagan ceremonials. Hopscotch is but one of many children's games which hold the secret of an ancient rite.

Other dance steps began in other ways. Many grew not from magic but from work. The sailor's hornpipe, arms raised above the head, imitates the way a sailor climbed the rigging of a bygone sailing ship. The Swedish weaving dance includes an imitation of a weaver's shuttle as it runs between the threads of the loom.

The dances of today owe much to rites and work of the past, but something to changing taste in castles, courts and ballrooms where dancing was an elegant pastime. Dance steps borrowed from uncultured peasants were adapted to suit refined courtly manners. Leaps became curtsies. A lively folk dance, tamed, became the famous minuet. Many "old time" dances popular today are country dances overlaid with elegance by ballroom dancing masters of previous centuries.

Perfected by the royal dancing masters at the court of France, the minuet reflected courtly fashions in its elegant and dainty steps.

Courtiers amusing King and nobles at Louis XIII's court donned grotesque masks and costumes to add excitement to their ballets.

16

Clothes, which differ in different lands and times, play their part in the story of the dance.

Witch doctors are the chief dancers of a savage tribe. To cure sickness or bring rain they don the dress and mask they think will represent a spirit bringing health or rain. Witch doctors and their audience believe the dancer becomes the spirit that he imitates. He "sheds" his own body for a body and a mind of superhuman power.

The purpose of such rites is long forgotten in the Western world. Yet people still perform folk dances in costumes which once had magic meaning. The fluttering handkerchiefs and jingling bells of the Morris dance, now "fancy dress," once played a vital part in a ritual dance to usher in the summer.

Courtiers were the dancers in a 17th century palace. To entertain their prince or king they put on masks and costumes simply to amaze and give delight. In a performance called "The Four Corners of the Earth," dancers wore exotic masks and costumes strange to European eyes.

No one believed the courtier became the black-amoor whose dress he wore. But costume lent extra excitement to the entertainment of the dance. It plays the same important part in modern ballets. In ballet, steps are ordinary movements changed by rhythm and emotion into art. The ballet story may be ordinary events selected to make an artistic tale. Ballet costume helps the dancer to lift both steps and story from everyday life into another world: one, not of ritual magic, but of artistic make-believe.

Through the centuries, costume has not only lent excitement to dance, it has helped to create dance steps. Traditional everyday dress, often heavy in colder climates, scanty in the tropics, plays its part in shaping folk dance, which itself affects all other social and spectacular dances.

Full skirts give rise to thrilling, whirling movements; heavy skirts and wooden shoes to stamping steps. Austrian mountaineers' shorts encourage the thigh-slapping *schuhplattler* dances. Russian cossacks' soft leather boots suggest the thrilling cobblers' kicks. Miners' clogs inspire dramatic clacking dances on the cobbled streets of mining towns.

Thus the story of dancing is not just a catalogue of steps or a museum of costumes. To understand it we must know where people live, how they live and why they change their ways of life.

Witch doctors who don a "spirit" costume for their dance believe that they themselves become a spirit, possessed of magic powers.

Cigarettes and savage masks, modern fancy dress and ancient magic costume mingle in the city streets of Trinidad at carnival time.

Different costumes may lead to different dances. Heavy dresses and hard-soled shoes helped to create staccato Spanish steps and rhythms.

Costumes designed to aid free leaping movements help these dancers' steps to match the freely flowing melodies of modern musical shows.

Savages mark all events in life with "magic" ritual. Masked New Guinea dancers initiate a boy into manhood. Jungle rites appear in city customs: a ball proclaims a debutante has "come of age."

Miming for Magic

Primitive man living in caves or jungles makes only the simplest tools to help him in his daily tasks. He is not, however, less intelligent than we are, if intelligence means ability to learn by experience.

One of the first things he notices is a number of events terrifyingly beyond his control. Friends and relatives die for no apparent reason. Trees and people are struck by lightning. The beasts that serve as food and clothing disappear.

To a savage, the sensible and obvious explanation of these events is that they are caused by powerful, invisible, often angry beings – spirits whose terrible "voices" he has heard in the storm. The savage knows from experience that he can appease a powerful warrior by certain acts and gifts. So it must be with the spirits. Thus rituals and sacrifices, serious, solemn, all-important, grow up to appease the spirits and obtain their blessing. We call such acts magic and condemn them as superstition. Yet we unconsciously perform our own ritual acts like tapping every third railing on a walk.

Primitive man developed ritual dance actions for every event in his life: for a birth, at the growing

Savages dance for events in tribal, as well as human, life. Here, Indians try to pacify their god as white men cast down his image.

Tribesmen the world over dance for many reasons. These once-warlike peoples all retain their warrior dances: (left) New Zealand Maoris, (right) a Borneo headhunter, (below) African Masai.

up of a young man, at a wedding, to cure the sick, to bury the dead. As well as a magic act, a boy's initiation dance is often a test of initiative and courage, to decide if the boy-man is fit to wield a spear as a member of his tribe. Girls have rites to prepare them for womanhood – debutante dances!

Rituals are also danced for every event in the community's life, both in war and peace. Maori war dances are particularly fierce, with the tempo marked by the beating of palms on thighs, the pulling of faces already grotesque with tattoo marks, and the defiant thrusting out of the tongue. Borneo headhunters do a victory dance, carrying their gruesome trophies to the main meeting house.

Most important peace time rites are dances to attract the savage hunters' quarry, and ensure the farmers a fruitful harvest. Often hunt and harvest depend on rain falling in a parched land. The Pueblo Indians have a complex rain dance. Drummers imitate thunder, pointing to the heavens, while dancers carry jointed sticks to portray lightning. When they have danced themselves into a frenzy, they drench themselves with water.

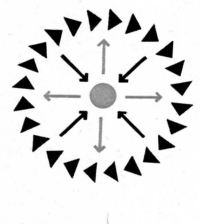

Diagram, left: Dancers encircling a "magic" object believe that power flows from it outward to the circle, then returns. Above: Present-day Congo tribesmen still perform their magic "rounds."

Magic dances are "imitative" (suggesting, by imitating desired actions, what the spirits should do to help the dancers) or "abstract."

Abstract dances often take the form of circles round a stone or wooden object, or witch doctor – something or someone believed to hold special magical power. As the dancers move in a ring, power is believed to flow from the object outwards to the ring and back again. The dance becomes so absorbing that dancers often feel neither fatigue nor pain. As they whirl around, the performers believe that they themselves become spirits.

These round dances date from earliest times. Unlike magic dances which grow up to overcome the problems of particular environments (such as the drought of deserts, the cold of northern climates), round dances are almost world-wide. They flourish wherever people believe that power can leave one object and enter another by magic.

Long after their ritual origin is forgotten, round dances go on. The maypole dance, still a spring festival, once circled a living tree, symbol of growth

Magic dances round objects of special power persist throughout the world. This Indian painting represents an Apache fire dance.

Ancient pagan rounds survive throughout the centuries. This 15th century Italian painting depicts angels in a round dance in the fields of Heaven. Today children still do "ring a ring o' roses."

and fertility for primitive farmers. Round dances invaded the ballrooms of 18th century Europe. Chain dances are still popular with the country people of eastern Europe, and survive today in the children's game of "Ring a Ring o' Roses."

Imitative dances play a vital part in the savage hunter's life. Before the chase, dancers disguise themselves as their animal quarry, perhaps a bear, a bison or an emu. Imitating the animal's movements, the dancers are hunted and "killed" by the rest of the tribe. This is "sympathetic" magic, which witches and sorcerers also use. They stick thorns and nails in little images of enemies, in the belief that their enemies will die.

Often, after a successful hunt, another imitative dance is done. This time it subdues the wrath of bear or bison spirits, angered by the hunt. Clothed in the dead bear's skin, the chief medicine man of a Sioux tribe skilfully copies the lumbering movements of the living animal. Thus the dead bear has magically "come alive" again, the bear spirits are appeased, and more good hunting is assured.

Indian "bison" dancers imitated bisons' movements in the drama of a chase. Successful hunting, they believed, would be assured.

Antler costumes worn both by Stone Age sorcerers and modern folk dancers hint at traditions unbroken through thousands of years.

Primitive man survives in the 20th century despite aeroplanes, radios, films and hydrogen bombs. In hidden corners of the world, the same age-old dances go on, for the same magical purposes. Son imitates father in steps trodden 20,000 years ago.

But year by year, explorer and miner invade the vast wild tracts of Australia, New Guinea, Central America. With them comes the way of life of Western civilization: Western science, Western arts, Western customs. With their coming disappears the way of life of primitive man: native magic, native arts and customs. Stored only in the the native mind, dances are the first art to vanish.

A famous explorer tells of just such a happening. He had penetrated the New Guinea forests to see a great tribal dance in which a tribe proudly displayed its wealth and traditions to the people living around. Its hospitality would cost so much that the host tribe would live in poverty for years.

But the explorer received a surprise. Instead of a savage ceremony, he was amazed to see a familiar New York Charleston. He soon understood why.

A native boy visiting Port Moresby on the coast had been in trouble with the police and was put in prison. There he saw a powerful display of white man's magic: an American musical film. Impressed beyond measure, he returned to the interior and taught the filmed dances to the rest of his tribe. Thus an age-old dance disappeared overnight.

So strong is the love of dancing in primitive people that when an old dance vanishes a new one often takes its place. An expert on Australia's native customs tells how she watched a shark dance, a pelican dance, a buffalo dance, followed by a vivid dance depicting a dog fight between a Japanese Zero aircraft and a British Spitfire.

Such examples tell of the world-wide use of dancing to record episodes from the past, often the legendary birth of a tribe from some animal. Among people who can neither read nor write, a dance may be the only record of an historical event. Thus there are Maori dances which imitate the paddling of canoes setting out from Polynesia for New Zealand, one of history's great migrations.

In the recent past, films and records have helped to drive out ancient native arts. Today, explorers armed with camera and tape recorder try to preserve these dances. They know that before their film has even been developed, the dances it records may be forgotten and beyond recall.

First watching experts, then copying their movements, youngsters in every land learn dance traditions, then pass them on to others.

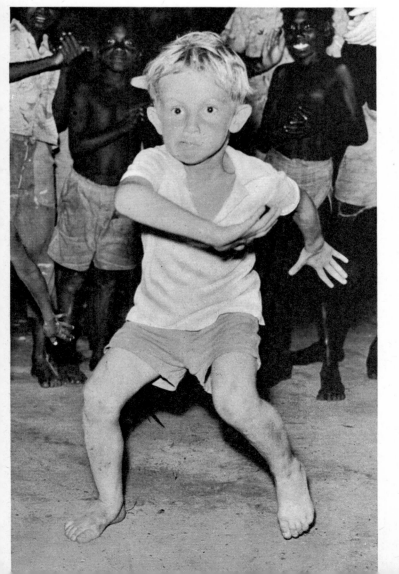

Left: An Australian farm manager's son displays the dances he has learned by watching aborigines perform them. Right: But primitive peoples, impressed by Western ways of life, are swiftly learning Western dances, Western music-making. Native arts soon vanish.

Dancing girls enlivened pharaohs' leisure hours in ancient Egypt.

24 From Egypt to Athens

Today primitive men are becoming rare. Five thousand years ago, civilized man himself was scarce. Probably he lived only in the Indus Valley of what we now call Pakistan, the Tigris-Euphrates Valley of Iraq, and the Nile Valley of Egypt.

In those fertile regions, farming first began. Controlled food production produced a surplus. People discovered this surplus could feed non-food-producing specialists able to make better tools for farmers. Settled farming villages supported more inhabitants, and became towns. Towns and villages joined to form a nation, held together by rulers.

As communities grew into the first civilizations, social laws and rituals developed with them. Magic became organized religion: witch doctors became priests, simple mud altars became towering *ziggurat*

temples. Ritual dancing became a complex part of the increasingly elaborate religious ceremonies.

In Egypt, priests or specially appointed temple dancers did ritual dances as part of the temple cult. One record tells how they danced around altars in patterns which represented the movements of heavenly bodies: a dance perhaps derived from the Tigris civilization where priests were skilled in studying the stars and planets.

The High Priest himself would act the role of the god Osiris in a great religious drama which magically helped to ensure the annual flooding of the Nile and a good harvest. At the elaborate funeral of a dead king, dancers ran to greet the procession and danced round the body to speed its spirit's journey to another world.

With ceremonial pomp a dead pharaoh (in the ship) is carried to his afterlife. Egypt's tomb and temple pictures testify to many rituals which flourished when civilized rule replaced barbarism.

The new class of leisured rulers, supported by the produce of farmers and craftsmen, entertained guests at banquets with the spectacle of skilful dancing girls. Ancient paintings show these dances, often much like the acrobatic *adagio* dances of a modern vaudeville show, where two men toss a woman in the air and juggle with her like a puppet. Egypt's dances also foreshadowed ballet.

We shall never know exactly how the Egyptians danced. Beautiful though they are, Egyptian wall paintings only show dancers in profile, for artists ignored perspective. But hieroglyphic writings reveal that dance steps had set and recognized names. Thus we do know that *organized* dancing was used for worship and pleasure throughout the land. Dancing had become a part of civilization.

Assyrian "military musicians" show that Egypt's civilization was not alone in organizing rhythmic sound and movement for its ends.

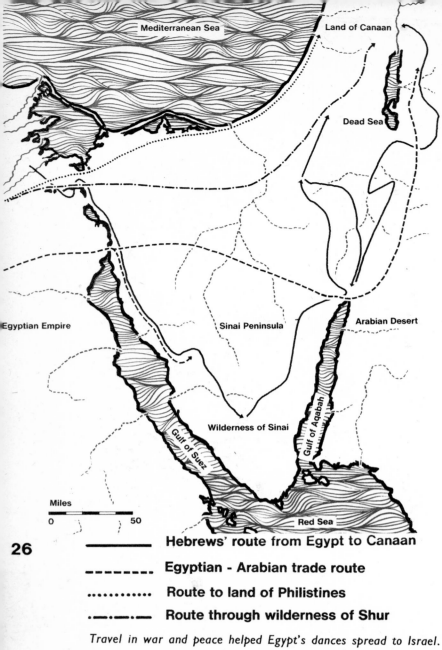

Mediterranean Sea

Land of Canaan

Dead Sea

Egyptian Empire

Sinai Peninsula

Arabian Desert

Gulf of Aqabah

Gulf of Suez

Wilderness of Sinai

Miles

0   50

Red Sea

26

————— **Hebrews' route from Egypt to Canaan**

――――― **Egyptian - Arabian trade route**

··········· **Route to land of Philistines**

·—·—·—· **Route through wilderness of Shur**

Travel in war and peace helped Egypt's dances spread to Israel.

No artist of ancient Israel depicted people. A modern attempt to recreate an ancient Jewish dancer (above) must owe much to traditions of dress and dance preserved by Yemenite tribesmen (below).

With trade, early civilizations throve and expanded. With wars they collapsed. But both trade routes and the routes of invading armies helped to spread ideas and arts, including the art of the dance.

Thus when the Children of Israel left the captivity of Egypt and began their 40-year trek through the Wilderness of Sinai, they took with them dances learned from their Egyptian overlords.

The Bible holds many examples of such dances. The Book of Exodus tells how, after the crossing of the Red Sea, "Miriam the prophetess, the sister of Aaron, took a timbrel in her hand and all the women went out after her with timbrels and with dances." Even David "danced before the Lord."

Israelites danced every year at celebrations in the spring, for the harvest festival and the Feast of Tabernacles. Though most dances took place in the Temple, Bible stories show they were folk dances, not just the special rites of priests.

But Salome's dance, best-known of all in the Bible, was a dance spectacle. The princess took the place of dancers paid to entertain at a feast. Her grim reward was St. John the Baptist's head.

Not even profile paintings, like those of Egypt, survive to show a dance of ancient Israel. Religion forbade Israelites to represent the human form in art. Yet this strange ban led artists of later ages to portray their own impressions of ancient Israel's dances. We are fortunate that many, ignorant of the past, depicted instead the dances of their own day, otherwise destined to vanish unremembered. The Bible still inspires painting and dance. Dame Ninette de Valois' ballet "Job," with music by Vaughan Williams, echoes the words of the Book of Job: "The happy and fortunate send forth their little ones like a flock, and their children dance."

Unaided by pictures from the past, we may still glean from the Bible clues as to how the Israelites danced – it seems in three main ways: 1. a ring dance round a central object, as round the Golden Calf; 2. a processional dance; and 3. a hopping, stamping dance. "Smite with thine hand and stamp with thy foot," says the Book of Ezekiel. Such stamping steps persist in the traditional feasts and weddings of Israel's Yemenite cousins.

Today dancing is widely popular among Israel's collective farms and settlements. Many dances have come from Russia and elsewhere. But the enduring Hebrew chants and the popularity of Yemenite dancing may help to recapture a lost tradition.

Tenth century artists showed King David as a 10th century monarch.   **27**

Salome: a 15th century artist showed her as a 15th century dancer. Ignorant of past dances, painters copied ones that they had seen.

The great dance drama festivals of Greece developed from simple dances round a threshing floor or altar. Unlike Egypt, democratic Athens held theatres planned to seat spectators by the thousand.

Greeks danced for many reasons. To maenads, devotees of Dionysus, the god of wine, wild steps and gestures were an act of worship.

Egypt's civilization grew up along the fertile banks of the Nile, a great waterway uniting a single great nation. Greek civilizations grew up in valleys. The mountains which separated valleys prevented their little city-states uniting to form one country.

In Egypt, one king commanded many thousand serfs, each an obedient ant in a gigantic anthill. In the small city-state of Athens, every individual played an important role. The people chose rulers to govern for, not over, them.

In Egypt, arts and sciences were dedicated to the king. In Athens, arts and sciences belonged to all. Egyptian priests had used their skill in science to keep themselves in power. Greek philosophers studied to find better ways of life for all. Dancing in Egypt was the privilege of priests, the entertainment of the king. In Greece it was the exercise of all, who strove, through dancing, to gain harmony of mind and body.

From the ancient days of Homer, dancing was held in high esteem. We read that Nausicaa led her maidens in a choral dance, that Ulysses was entertained by dancing at Alcinous' court. The writer Lucian declared: "The most noble and greatest personages in every city are the dancers [who] applaud themselves more upon their dexterity . . . than on their nobility, their posts of honour and the dignities of their forefathers."

Greeks had dances for worship, for everyday events in life and for war. Indeed the art of drama grew from the religious *dithyrambos*, a ritual spring song whose accents dictated the rhythms of a ritual dance. Dancing floors, called *orchestras*, formed the first stages. On them a chorus mimed and danced

and sang. Greek drama joined poetry, music and dance to tell one story in a way admired and imitated to the present day.

Everyday dances included ones for courtship. The Greek historian Herodotus tells how Cleisthenes offered his daughter to the most accomplished dancer. The rivals were Megacles and Hippocleides. But Megacles was the victor, for Hippocleides danced away his bride by dancing acrobatically for applause. To the Greeks, dancing meant more than a mere show of skill.

It played a great part in educating young people, for the Greeks believed healthy bodies mattered as much as well-trained minds. Even the army danced: a dance which "inflamed courage and gave strength to persevere in the paths of honour and valour."

The Greeks borrowed steps from Egypt and other lands, developed dances for many purposes. But to a Greek of Athens, a dance for worship, love or war was something more. It was a way to build a fitter body and a sounder mind.

Dance dramas began as solemn, tragic rites. Later, comedies grew up. Comic actor-dancers disguised themselves as birds and beasts.

29

Athletes and soldiers danced. Greeks thought dancing, demanding control of brain and muscles, created a balanced mind and body.

Linked arms of modern kolo (above), and ancient trata (below), give proofs of an east European dance tradition 3,000 years old.

Admirers of the Athenian way of life have made many attempts to discover *how* Athenians danced to build a better mind and body.

Proofs of past dances are hard to find. Ancient pictures of the dance known as *kolo, horo, trata,* in different eastern European lands, reveal a dance which peasants still perform. Tradition says the *trata's* linking arms copy the legend of Theseus leading youths and maidens safely from the Cretan labyrinth. But such chain dances are a form of ancient round, and date from long before the time of classic Greece.

No dances done in Greece today appear to be the same as those which classic sculptures show. How, then, can ancient steps be recreated? One expert, Maurice Emmanuel, collected thousands of vase and sculpture pictures in the hope that they would hold the vital clues. He said the human

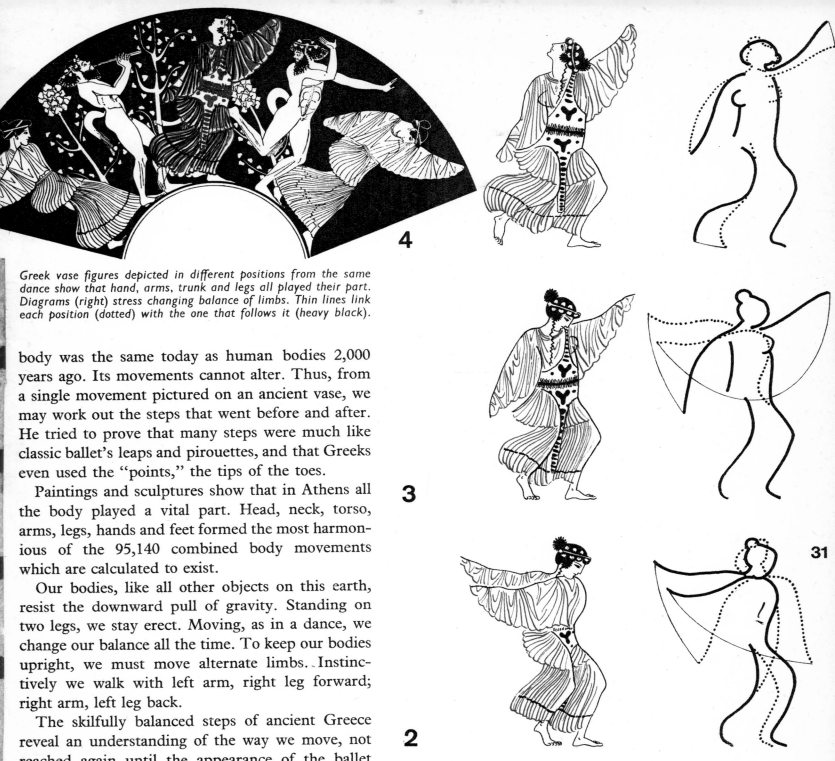

Greek vase figures depicted in different positions from the same dance show that hand, arms, trunk and legs all played their part. Diagrams (right) stress changing balance of limbs. Thin lines link each position (dotted) with the one that follows it (heavy black).

body was the same today as human bodies 2,000 years ago. Its movements cannot alter. Thus, from a single movement pictured on an ancient vase, we may work out the steps that went before and after. He tried to prove that many steps were much like classic ballet's leaps and pirouettes, and that Greeks even used the "points," the tips of the toes.

Paintings and sculptures show that in Athens all the body played a vital part. Head, neck, torso, arms, legs, hands and feet formed the most harmonious of the 95,140 combined body movements which are calculated to exist.

Our bodies, like all other objects on this earth, resist the downward pull of gravity. Standing on two legs, we stay erect. Moving, as in a dance, we change our balance all the time. To keep our bodies upright, we must move alternate limbs. Instinctively we walk with left arm, right leg forward; right arm, left leg back.

The skilfully balanced steps of ancient Greece reveal an understanding of the way we move, not reached again until the appearance of the ballet masters two centuries ago. Greek artists show Greek dancers in the *arabesque*, a pose demanding skilled control of every member of the body for balance on one foot alone. Aware of balance creating beauty in movement, Greek artists could also show imbalance in a drunken satyr's dance, his left arm, left leg forward; right arm, right leg back.

Despite the scholars' studies, no one will ever know exactly how people performed a classic dance. But Greek dancing matters less to us for what it was than what it was thought to be, about four centuries ago, when half-remembered arts of Greece inspired the European birth of ballet.

Above: Shown here decayed with age a century ago, Hindu temples still shelter age-old Hindu dances performed as acts of worship.

Left: Eastern travel depicted on an ancient Greek vase suggests that India's dances went from Greece to India, or India to Greece.

From Tibet to Tokyo

The story of the Western world, from classic Greece up to the present day, is one of wars and famines. But also it is one of ways of life which changed as Western man invented new ideas and machines to improve the world in which he lived.

The story of the Eastern world is different: a story also of wars and famine, but in a continent where men accepted problems, seeking less to solve them than to find relief in religious meditation. Thus in most Eastern lands, ways of life and art have remained the same for many centuries.

Hindu dancing, unlike that of Greece, is today as it was perhaps 2,000 years ago – the oldest dance tradition of the cultured world. We have no need to guess the movements of the gestures, frozen in time on temple carvings centuries ago.

A Hindu dance, like that of Greece, is one of mime and gesture. Perhaps, when Alexander the Great invaded India in 327 B.C. he introduced from Greece some of the dances of that land. Or possibly, some centuries before his time, the dance of India had spread to Greece, where it survives to this day in works of art alone.

Dancing is deeply rooted in Hindu life and thought. Traditional belief says the god Siva set the world in motion with a dance, a belief perhaps derived from the world's first cultured people whose priests declared the stars moved in a dance. In southern India, temple sculptures show the god as *Nataraja* (King of Dancers). Statuettes with many arms perpetuate his gestures. Others depict Parvati, Siva's wife, inventor of the softer, women's dances.

The steps and gestures of all Hindu dances performed today derive from a book: Bharata's *Natya Sastra* (the science of dancing). Its Sanskrit manuscript was written down about the time that Christ was born. Its teachings fade in the vast distances of ancient myth. The gods, tradition says, entrusted the sage Bharata with the secret of the dance. Bharata's writings, some still preserved on palm leaves, make Hindus the only people in the world to have a semi-sacred book as a text book of art.

A Hindu dance, performed in temples, was not a popular pursuit for leisure hours. Skilled artists, through its movements, had to imitate the thoughts and feelings, joys and sorrows, of gods and men.

Left: Centuries-old statuettes of Siva show the dance that "set the world in motion." Below: Unchanged since Siva's statuettes were made, Hindu dances preserve both art traditions and beliefs.

Hindu dancing may well be the most *complete* on earth. Each part of the body has its special movements. To learn how to control them takes more than a dancing lesson once a week.

Temple dancing girls were *devadasi*, servants of the god. Their lives were dedicated to the dance, which was an act of worship, not entertainment. Myths which temple carvings illustrate show *devadasis* as winged nymphs, *asparas*, strangely like the dancing angels of early Christian belief.

Today, few temple dancing girls remain, but girls still learn their art. The best age to begin is eight. The would-be pupil must find a *guru* (teacher), his home perhaps a village far away. If he accepts her, she becomes a member of his household, like an apprentice in a medieval town. The teacher then instructs his pupil in the knowledge he has gained from an unbroken chain of son and father links which stretches back perhaps for 80 generations.

He teaches her the movements of the *anga*, "limbs": head, hands, arms, chest, hips, legs, feet; those of the *pratyanga*, "intermediate parts": neck, shoulders, palms, back, stomach, thighs, ankles, knees, elbows, wrists; those of the *upanga*, "lesser limbs": eyes, eyebrows, eyelashes, cheeks, nose, lips, teeth, tongue, chin, mouth, jaw. The *Natya Sastra* describes positions for them all, nine for the head, eight glances of the eye, six movements of the eyebrows, four of the neck and at least 4,000 *mudras*: picture gestures of the hands.

A *mudra* may imitate an actual object: a swimming fish, a flying bird, a lotus flower in bloom. It also shows an abstract mood: love, hate, fear, surprise. A skilful dancer can tell a story without words.

The dance itself is in accordance with nine moods or *rasas*, which the *Natya Sastra* has described: fury, fear, love, heroism, comedy, pathos, admiration, revulsion, meditation. As in all ritual dances, music and dance are one. Unlike Western ballet, dancer and musicians do not repeat a ready-made pattern of steps and notes. They *improvize* their complex rhythm: drums, singer, dancer's ankle bells all miraculously blend to invoke the gods.

Many temple dancers in the past abused their calling, using gestures to display their bodies, not to express religious feeling. To Western eyes the true beauty of the dance remained obscure until the present century. Thanks largely to the enthusiasm of Pavlova, the famous Russian ballerina, Hindu dancing today claims countless admirers.

34

bird in flight

perching pigeon

deer's head

Almost every muscle of the body plays its part in Hindu temple dances. The devadasi, temple dancers, must master 4,000 mudras: picture-gestures of the hands which tell a story without words.

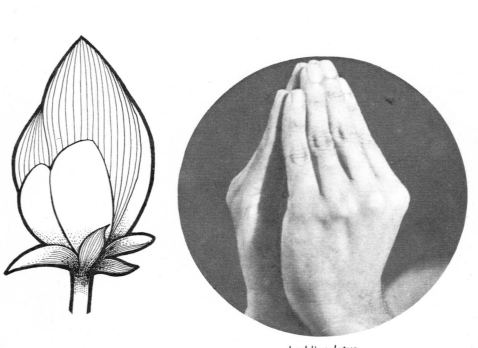

budding lotus

lotus in bloom

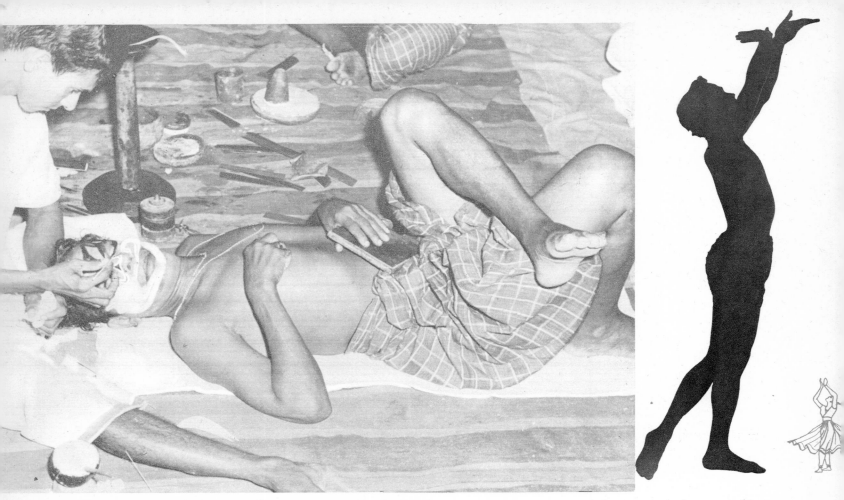

Hindu dancing means worship as well as entertainment. During make-up, a Kathakali *actor meditates on Krishna, whose part he plays.*

 We have talked as if all Indian dances were one. Four great schools of dancing have developed from one common source: two in the south, two in the north. Each has rather different versions of the *Natya Sastra* gestures.

The oldest is south India's *Bharata Natya* school. *Bharata* may derive from words which mean "outward expression of spiritual feeling," "melody" and "rhythm." This is the dance that temple sculptures show. Once, only *devadasis* performed it. Many people still think of it as solely meant for women. But some of the greatest dancers who have helped revive its fame are men. As in all Indian dance, hands play an important part. Their rich gesture language can portray emotions, moods or objects. So beautiful are these *mudras* in themselves that one can talk of "dancing hands."

Kathakali (danced drama) comes from India's south-west coast. Performers wear billowing skirt-like garments inspired by clothes which Portuguese settlers wore 400 years ago. But *Kathakali* itself may be much older. Three kinds of characters, the virtuous, heroic, devilish, enact the life of gods and demons. Originally, only male dancers took part; *Kathakali* would test the stamina of the strongest.

Before it even starts, trained artists spend four hours applying the performer's complicated make-up. In the performance, which may last all night, mime plays a tremendous role. Performers must perfect nine separate eyeball movements. Unlike the temple dances, *Kathakali* appeals to all. It takes place in the open air, upon a platform where a large lamp adds its softly flickering light to the mysterious effect of costume and make-up.

From Manipur in north-east India come the soft, graceful *Manipuri* dances depicting the charming legends of the god Krishna. The land of Manipur, "created as a dance floor for the gods," is rich in folk dance. Rabindranath Tagore, playwright and poet, used its dances when he helped revive forgotten native arts.

Kathak is also from the north: a court, not a religious dance, although it tells the legends of the gods. It flourished in the time of Moslem conquerors who, unlike Hindus, looked on dancing as entertainment. Thus its purpose is akin to Western ballet. Its elegant, exciting, lightning turning steps are not seen elsewhere in India. Artists who painted the famous Persian miniatures often depicted scenes of *Kathak* dancers entertaining princes.

Silhouettes (left-right): Kathak *turning movement,* Manipuri *"Krishna" playing flute, bowed-leg* Kathakali *stance,* Bharata Natya *attitude.*

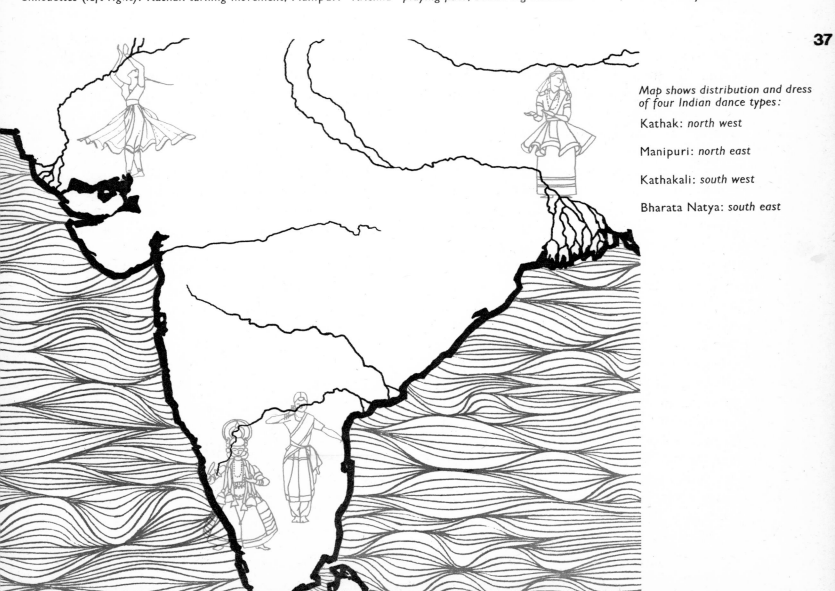

Map shows distribution and dress of four Indian dance types:

Kathak: *north west*

Manipuri: *north east*

Kathakali: *south west*

Bharata Natya: *south east*

Religious symbols of the Buddha spread overland with missionary monks who also helped make Indian art and dancing better known.

Dance gestures in India and south-east Asia seem much alike. They are, for the story of the dance in Burma, Thailand, Malaya, Indonesia is the story of the spread of Indian arts: by sea from south India, by overland routes from the north.

Well over 1,000 years ago, south India's warrior kings invaded Ceylon. Later, ambitious merchants spread peacefully to Burma, taking trade and Indian

Ships and sea trade first carried Indian arts to the island of Ceylon where Kandyan dancers (right) perform dances of Indian origin.

4

38

In China, a land where lions are unknown, performers imitate these animals in dances first learned perhaps from Indian missionaries.

2

1 In Tibet, stronghold of present-day Buddhism, masked Lama dances which are still performed may pre-date even Hindu dancing arts.

modes of life. They later settled in Thailand, Malaya, Indonesia. With them went Indian dancing. Indian *mudras* often became forgotten, but east Asia's supple gestures clearly reveal the dance art that originally inspired them.

At least 2,000 years ago, north India's Buddhist missionary monks spread north into Tibet, east into China, Korea and Japan. They also carried with them Indian ways of life. Thanks to these Buddhist priests, China and Japan preserve ancient dances long forgotten in their native land. China's Lion Dance, done in a lion-less land, derives from India. Japan's strange *Bugaku* masks and dances have been preserved perhaps 2,000 years. Only crumbling sculptures remain in India to reveal the land which gave *Bugaku* birth.

3

Japan's Gigaku masks, like the Bugaku dances, bear witness to arts derived from India where, many centuries ago, they were forgotten.

5 Thailand dancers enact the roles of Hanuman, the monkey god, and other characters from the Ramayana, India's great religious epic.

6

Tradition has preserved Hindu dance gestures as faithfully in the remote Indonesian island, Bali, as in parts of India itself.

Though India's dances are best-known, the rest of Asia has its own. Yet China has few dances. Unlike India, its people do not worship dancing gods.

The Chinese care less about the lives of gods than about the deeds of men. Thus the human stories of the Chinese classic theatre grew up, fusing music, mime and words as Greek plays had also done. Older by far than opera – the nearest thing we have to it today – Chinese theatre began before the Normans conquered England.

Instead of comedy and tragedy, its plays tell of civil life or war. Actors wear painted faces – shiny for heroes, dull for villains. 200 differently made-up faces portray as many types of character.

Its make-up perhaps links Chinese theatre with Indian *Kathakali* plays. But the simple, imitative gestures of a Chinese play are far removed from India's complex gesture language of the dance. Yet Chinese actors must be skilled in acrobatic dance. A "fighting" actor balances and whirls and turns cartwheels on the stage. A Chinese sage once said: "An actor without ability to dance is like a wrestler without strength."

Enriched by Chinese themes, dance dramas grew up in Japan in Emperor Ashikaya Shogun's reign. Five hundred years ago, the *Nō* plays, still produced today, were first performed. Three hundred years ago, *Kabuki* plays were born. Their dramas still attract more people than the courtly *Nō*. *Nō* means "skill." *Kabuki* may mean "frolic."

Nō actors wear a mask; *Kabuki* actors paint one on their faces. After A.D. 1643, when a ban forbade women to act, men grew highly skilled in female roles and still play them today. The actor-dancers of Japan are graceful and subtle. Their skilful mime can "turn" a fan into a butterfly. Sometimes their subtle movements are so slight, we might not consider them a dance at all. Yet the audience appreciates their skill and shouts its approval.

Little less graceful, much more energetic than the theatre dances of Japan, are Asia's gymnastic dances. China's *T'ai chi Ch'uan*, at first sight like a shadow-boxing match, is an exercise designed to strengthen the body and "cure it of disease." *Penchak*, popular in Indonesia's islands, means "evasion." Its movements remind us of *Judo* (way of weakness), the wrestling skill of Japan.

War dances in the West built up the dancer's strength and helped him to subdue his foe by force. A lightning movement of a *Penchak* dancer's wrist can turn defeat to victory. Eastern dances are a mode of combat won by subterfuge, not strength.

Gymnastic, acrobatic Eastern dances provide a keep-fit pastime for those who do them, an entertainment for the ones who watch.

40

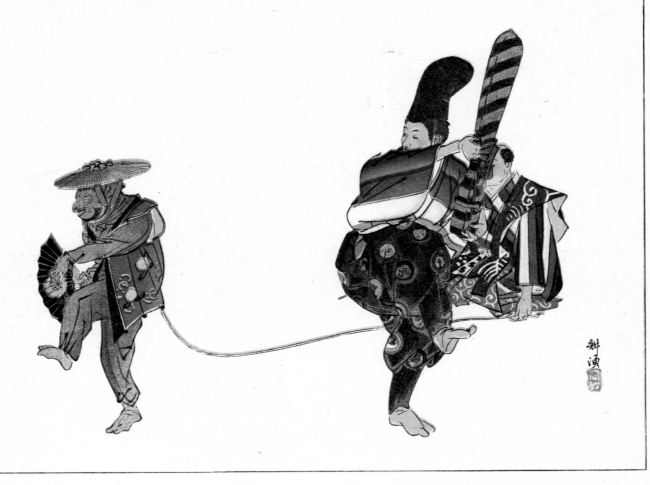

Above: Actor-dancers in a Kabuki play, most popular drama of Japan. Japanese dance dramas are derived from China's opera plays.

Below: Splendidly costumed Chinese performers re-enact with mime and music the tales of Chinese emperors who ruled 500 years ago.

Leaders like Augustus Caesar (left) led Roman armies to distant lands (above). Conquest and captured wealth inspired the building of triumphal arches (below, foreground) and giant sports arenas (below, skyline), where Rome's citizens celebrated victories and spent their leisure hours.

Heathen or Heavenly ?

Unchanging ways of life helped to preserve the arts of Eastern lands for many centuries. In Western lands, new empires, new religions arose: ways of life and art changed with them. Rome's armies subdued Greece. But Rome, the conqueror nation, borrowed many Grecian arts.

With wealth and leisure time derived from conquest and slave labor, many Roman citizens frequently visited places of entertainment. Vast arenas held audiences of over 200,000 people. Many spectators were visitors to Rome and ignorant of the Latin tongue; to satisfy them, gesture-dancing, borrowed from the Greeks, became a flourishing art. People of all nations could follow mimed stories.

These *mimes* (the word meant "play" and "player") were scenes drawn from daily life. Performed between the main spectacles, they gave the chief performers rest, like a turn in modern music hall or cabaret. A plain cloth, *siparum*, drawn across the large stage, helped to focus attention on the gestures of a solo mimic actor. Later, a mime called *exodium*, or exit piece, would end the performance. At annual games dedicated to the goddess Flora, mimes were the only form of entertainment.

Patterned in mosaic is a Roman chariot race – one of the gigantic spectacles which became more popular than skilful dance or mime.

In Augustus Caesar's time, admirers of Bathyllus and Pylades, both famous mimes, once came to blows discussing who was greater. Rebuked for this by Augustus, Pylades replied: "You should be pleased, Caesar, that the people are interested in our quarrels rather than your actions." Emperors encouraged spectacles to take people's minds off their deeds.

With frequent spectacles, people grew tired of skilful mime, and clamored for crude display: striptease dancing, gladiators' combats, martyrs thrown to lions. Dancing grew debased. The poet Cicero wrote that to dance a man must be either drunk or mad. But Lucian defended the dance. He said all sacred rites in Greece were incomplete without it.

When the Christian Church became more powerful in Rome, it frowned on dancing partly for what it had become, but also because people still danced to worship pagan gods: the *Salii*, in which the priests of Mars copied their leader's rhythmic, marching steps; the *Lupercalia*, in which half-naked youths danced through the streets whipping passers-by; the festival of Flora, where dancers were decked with flowers – a ritual which lives on in May Day festivals still celebrated in modern Europe.

This "Dance of the Seasons" may have been a religious Roman rite intended to ensure a fertile seed-time or to celebrate a harvest.

The first Christians despised both Greek and Roman ritual. But the Christian Church adapted pagan dances for its own worship. Wisely it made use of ancient customs since it could not root them out.

Before Christ's death and resurrection, a Greek religion had taught that there was an afterlife. When a man died, Greeks danced in rings to mark his passage safely through the underworld to the fields of the blessed. Early Christians borrowed this idea and performed a lively funeral dance to celebrate a dead man's birth into everlasting life. They believed the dead would be united to throngs of angels who, with circling movements, worshipped the Creator.

Dances in churches began to imitate the angels' heavenly rings. An early leader of the Church, Clement of Alexandria, approved and said: "Then shalt thou dance in a ring together with the Angels, around Him Who is without beginning or end."

Sacred dances also celebrated anniversaries of martyrs' deaths. People thus paid them homage and enlisted aid, for martyrs' relics were believed to have special powers to drive out sickness and evil.

Such rites were performed in several ways: by one or many dancers, to hopping, leaping steps, as a "round" or a procession, to solo song or choir.

Processions still survive in many parts of the world. In a Sicilian town, slow-hopping dancers bear large wooden carvings of Our Lady through the streets for many hours. Masked revellers and "giants" parading in the Carnival of Nice and in the Mardi Gras festival in New Orleans show that although pagan rites were Christianized almost 2,000 years ago, their memories still linger.

Throughout its history, the Christian Church has had from time to time to clip fresh shoots of half-forgotten pagan rites. In the sixth century, for example, the Festival of Fools flourished in many countries: a strange mixture of Christian worship and pagan ceremonial. Held as a memorial to the ass and mule, its purpose was to raise the lowly. At another festival boy bishops were elected and choristers and congregation danced in the church aisles.

The Church leaders always suspected that dancing sheltered heathen practices. When men and women danced together, as they do today, the Church condemned them for imitating "heathen dances devoted to Bacchus and Dionysus." For centuries no great new European way of dancing evolved for, after the Roman Empire fell apart, only the half-hostile Church fostered the art of dance.

Festival parades derive from ancient Christian dance processions. These "giants" derive from pagan ceremonial dances even older.

After a dance to purify them, hooded "devils" sit outside this Venezuelan church until its priest declares that they may enter.

45

Below: "Dancing maniacs" depicted 400 years ago. Cramps, caused by ergotism, made the victims' limbs jerk beyond control.

Right: In 1374 pilgrimage routes became "dancing maniac" processions where pilgrims entered ergot-stricken towns (in brackets).

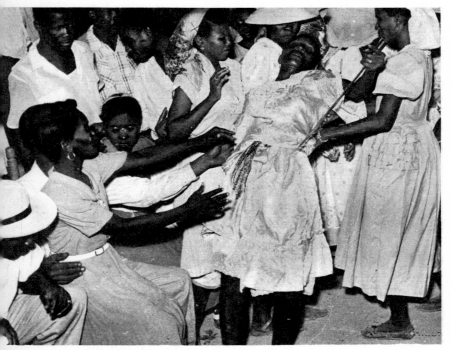

A story is told in Kolbigk, Saxony, that in the year 1021 three women and 15 men formed a circle to dance in a churchyard on Christmas Eve. The priest bade them come to Christmas Mass, but they went on dancing. The brother of one of the women dancers seized her arm to make her stop. The arm remained in his hand, but there was no blood – a sure sign of witchcraft. Still they danced. The priest excommunicated them from the Church and commanded them to dance for a year without ceasing. When the year was over they were hip-deep in the ground. Four then died, and the others went on trembling for the rest of their lives.

In 1518 a dancing "epidemic" broke out in the German town of Strasbourg. People danced through the streets day and night until they dropped from exhaustion. The town authorities set aside halls, then two squares, and provided music for the dancers.

The devotees of strange religious cults dance hysterically as a way of worship. (Above) Voodoo priestess, (below) dancing dervishes.

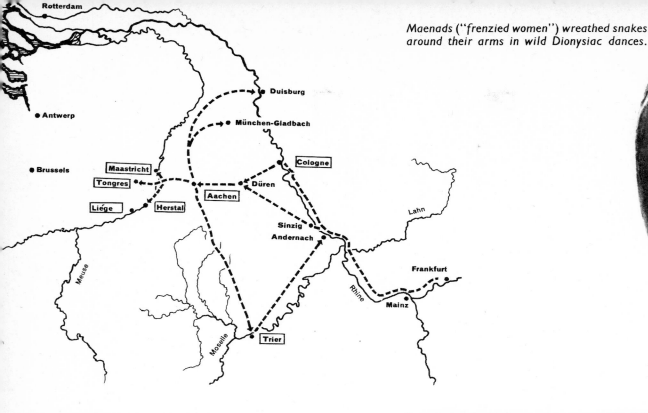

Maenads ("frenzied women") wreathed snakes around their arms in wild Dionysiac dances.

Many died, but others, sprinkled with holy water in St. Vitus' name, were cured. Those who survived were given small crosses and red shoes. Inspired by this event, Hans Andersen wrote *The Red Shoes*.

These stories of Kolbigk and Strasbourg are only two examples of European epidemic dancing.

To the medieval Church, these outbreaks were merely proof that dancing and evil went hand in hand. The Church thought devils had entered the dancers' bodies, or that St. Antony had punished them by making them dance in penitence for sins.

Today, scientific medicine has a better explanation. Medieval European peasants ate rye bread. Wet summers encourage the fungus ergot to grow on ears of rye. Rye bread made with ergot is poisonous. An ergot-poisoned man may lose control of his limbs which wildly jerk about. This in itself looks like a grotesque dance. It must have seemed still more so when, as in 1374, processions of dancing pilgrims passed through ergot-affected towns and became processions of "dancing maniacs."

Modern medicine also suggests that famine, plague and war, all frequent in the Middle Ages, led to mass nervousness which people relieved by dancing till exhausted – another type of "mania."

In all ages and lands hysterical dances have been known, from the maenads of Greece, the whirling dervishes of Moslem lands, to the *Ketchak* dance of Bali. Even the modern Western world has seen examples when teenagers, hysterically excited by a rock 'n' roll film, have danced in cinema aisles.

Arms raised, seated cross-legged on the ground, participators in Bali's Ketchak dance sway to and fro until they fall into a trance.

To those who lived when man was ignorant of medicine, when plague often cut life short, Christianity had brought new hope: the hope of happiness after death. To many, life meant hardship to be endured as preparation for the life to come.

This way of looking at life and death remained unchanged throughout the so-called Dark Ages and into the Middle Ages that followed. The fine churches themselves hinted at the glory of eternal life in contrast to the meanness of peasants' earthly dwellings in the world around – a world of warring Popes and princes where plague and famine struck.

Slowly, order arose from the chaos created when the Roman Empire fell. Peace-loving merchants gained power from warring princes. Trade increased. More people became better off. Life became worth living. Death, still all too frequent, all too sudden, now seemed a prison, not a release.

In this atmosphere a strange dance grew up. It had no definite steps. It happened, not in reality, but in the minds of medieval writers, on the church walls painted by artists. It was the Dance of Death.

Pictures showed Death, often as a skeleton, leading a dance of kings and peasants, young and old. Worse than any dancing mania, none could escape it. Rich and poor, noble and base-born, all must one day join together in the fatal dance.

Although this *danse macabre's* fame comes from medieval Europe, its origins lie farther afield, perhaps in the ancient history of the Arabs, for *macabre* comes from the Arabic *makâbr*: "churchyards."

Linked with the Dance of Death, dances were actually performed in medieval churchyards. They kept alive a heathen tradition. Before the coming of Christianity, German pagans believed the dead became demons or *wilis*, ever ready to drag the living down into the grave. A legend of these *wilis* later became the theme for "Giselle," the famous ballet.

Despite the prohibition of the Church, dances in churchyards kept alive this superstition. They were both for and against the dead: to give them repose and to protect the living from the dead's attempts to drag them down. Scantily clad, masked dancers would beat drums and perform boisterous, three-step hopping dances in a circle.

The feasting, merriment and dance (from right to left around a coffin) accompanying an Irish funeral feast or wake, remind us of these ancient customs. We confidently think that magic ritual in the modern world is dead. Perhaps we should not be too sure.

48

Secure in walled garden of court and castle, medieval nobles (left) passed peaceful leisure hours. Torn by plague and war, the world outside inspired the Dance of Death and paintings, represented below. Above: "Giselle," the famous ballet, bears a relic of this grim age in its story of the dead spirits who ensnare the living.

In bygone centuries, peasants at a village fair amused themselves by wrestling, climbing greasy poles and, above all, by dancing.

Basse Danse and Bunny Hug

The worst horrors of the Middle Ages failed to stop people dancing for joy. In an age when television was unknown, everyone created his own entertainment. Peasants flocked to town and village festivals and fairs to meet, to talk, to dance.

Primitive men had danced a purposeful ritual. Medieval peasants danced more to make themselves happy and to meet their future wives and husbands. Primitive dances had been performed by men or women only. Peasant dances were social dances for the enjoyment of both men and women.

Yet the names of medieval peasant dances, some of which survive today, remind us that they too began as ritual. "Reipe, Reipe, Garste" from the Netherlands means "Ripe, Ripe, Rye." Once it must have been a magic harvest dance. "The Seven Jumps," famous throughout Europe, derives from leaps to make the corn grow high.

Village green and city ballroom may seem worlds apart. But medieval peasant dances link both savage past and civilized present. Ancient magic rounds became the medieval *carole*, *branle*, the 18th century *cotillon and quadrille*, the square dance still popular in dance halls at the present day.

Ritual pantomimes performed to make things happen in savage settlements led in time to peasant social dances, done for pleasure.

Left: A lively peasant dance engraved by Albrecht Dürer in 1514. Right: Folk dances photographed today reveal vitality as great as ever.

Once a dance has journeyed from the prehistoric past to present-day civilization, it often travels "back" again. "Anna van Duinen," the Dutch folk dance, is "*en avant deux*," a *quadrille* dance-leader's call which country people had mispronounced. A peasant dance first inspired the ballroom *quadrille: quadrille* in turn inspired "Anna van Duinen."

What were the medieval peasant dances like, to which we owe so much today? Unrestrained by cumbersome clothes or rules of etiquette, a village dance was frequently a wild affair. In the south German *ländler*, men swung their partners round and flung them in the air. In other lands a social dance was tamer, but it was always an opportunity for everyone to let himself go.

In Dark Age Europe there was little difference in the way that all men danced. But by the Middle Ages, nobles lived a life very different from peasants. Polite, refined, they frowned on wildly abandoned couple dances. Even in 1816, the poet Byron criticized a vigorous, gay new ballroom dance, borrowed from the peasant *ländler*. It was the waltz. Yet, despite their critics, peasant dances were ever entering court and ballroom to begin new fashions.

Lively folk dance steps forever found their way from countryside to court and ballroom to create new fashions and enliven old ones.

52

Free from rules of etiquette, unrestricted by the shape of ball-room floors, lively peasant rounds flourished outside city walls.

Courtly fashions by no means only led to feebler versions of folk dances. What a folk dance lost in gaiety behind the castle walls it gained in artistry, partly born of courtly codes of chivalry.

These codes of "courtly love" evolved in 12th century castles of Provence. They linger still. Today men stand aside to let a lady pass, or rise to greet her. Medieval rules of courtly love declared it was unseemly for noblemen and noblewomen to frisk about like peasants. Thus when a peasant dance entered a castle its steps were "tamed," grew grave and slow, deliberate and more precise.

Courtly fashions also affected the way that nobles danced. Unlike a peasant, a nobleman need not wear working clothes as his everyday dress. Indeed his finery proclaimed his rank in life. By 1400, nobles sported short doublets and tight-fitting hose. Some wore shoes with pointed toes two feet long. Women trailed trains made of five yards of material. These made free movement far from easy and helped to keep dances staid and grave.

But fashions changed, and dances with them. By 1588 the stately *basse dance* was outdated. We learn this from *Orchésographie* by Thoinot Arbeau (pen name of Jehan Tabouret, Canon of Langres in France). His book was planned to teach "the honorable exercise of dancing." It tells of other dances since forgotten: the stately *pavane*, the lively *galliard* which followed the *pavane* in a suite of dances, the *volta*, perhaps one ancestor of the waltz.

Thoinot Arbeau's book tells us more of bygone dances than the books of dancing masters, more anxious to advertise steps of their own devising. These teachers first gained important posts in Italy 600 years ago. They played the chief part in turning peasants' rounds and couple dances into works of art. Created from a Poitou peasant round 300 years ago, the minuet is easily the most famous and elaborate of such dances. One dancing master wrote 60 pages on a description of its opening bow alone.

Inside medieval castle walls, codes of chivalry and courtly love transformed leaping peasant dances into staid and slower steps.

Shown below: The modern square dance is a country dance, refined and made more intricate by dancing masters who lived 200 years ago.

At court balls, country dances in time became as popular as minuets. In rectangular rooms, country "longways" dances like the "hey-for-three" (above left) were more easily performed than "rounds." But in 1800 rounds like the allemande (above right) were still a ballroom fashion.

In 1789 revolution swept away the court of France. With it disappeared its courtly social dances: *gavotte* and minuet. In their place, revolutionaries danced the *carmagnole* round the grim guillotine and tree of liberty. In France, 500 years of etiquette, born of the rules of courtly love, came to an end.

With less bloodshed, the same thing was taking place in other nations. Once, a castle baron had protected villagers from rival lords. As centuries passed, his noble heirs grew less useful but little less wealthy. But by 1850, prosperous merchant-manufacturers and oppressed peasants between them had wrested power from many royal rulers. The way was paved for democratic government.

All over Europe ideas of liberty were changing people's ways of life. Even before 1800, Europe's music, poetry and painting revealed ideas of freedom which replaced ideals of courtly refinement. Poets wrote of natural scenes. They borrowed less from the formal learning of long-dead Greek and Roman poets, more from the simplicity of peasants' folk songs. Despite the disapproving dancing masters, simple country steps grew more popular than the complex patterns of the minuet. So-called country dances became fashionable at elegant city balls.

Most popular of all new dances was the waltz. It owes its name to the latin *volvere*, to turn. Its ancestor, the *ländler* came from *das Landl*, an

Below and below right: The waltz, derived from Austria's peasant ländler, swept 19th century ballrooms like a "dancing mania."

Celebrations marked an anniversary of the French Revolution. The Revolution brought to an end 500-year-old courtly dance traditions.

Austrian mountain region. The *ländler* was already ancient when changing ways of city life gained for it sudden fame which spread throughout the world.

Musicians, moving on barges down the Danube, playing at fairs and inns, first carried its gay tunes to Vienna. There, where everyone from count to kitchen maid danced together at carnival time, the waltz began its conquest of the world.

Smooth dance floors instead of rough ground, city shoes instead of hob-nailed boots led to faster, smoother steps. City manners, still inspired by dying courtly ways of life, gracefully ignored the *ländler* custom of tossing the girls high.

By 1790, Vienna's waltz was all the rage in German towns. Seven years later Paris could boast almost 700 dance halls, chiefly built to satisfy the new craze. Schubert, Chopin, Strauss helped to spread the fame of waltz tunes. First Europe, then America was swept by this "dancing mania," which lasted almost 100 years. The United States created the *Boston*, Germany the *schottische:* both new versions of the 19th century's most famous dance.

But 19th century rivals faced the waltz. Chief of these was the *polka*, from Central Europe. Nineteenth century railways and revolutions helped to bring to Western Europe's eyes the dances of many European nations: the Hungarian *czardas*, the Italian *tarantella*, Russia's *gopak*, Spain's *flamenco*.

Right: The waltz became world famous. This 19th century cartoon suggests how much it owed its fame to a Johann Strauss waltz tune.

Inspired by the River Danube...

Strauss writes "The Blue Danube."

Everyone waltzes to its tunes...

Russians

Africans

Laplanders

Everyone visits Johann Strauss...

to pay him homage.

Right: Hundreds performed waltz, schottische and polka in enormous dance halls which replaced the private ballrooms of the past.

Native drummers (left) and "darkies" in a New York Charleston (right) reveal the lively rhythms of Negro music, Negro dancing.

Africa ▸ work songs spirituals and blues minstrels and ragtime

Scots, Irish, English hymns and ballads

Scots, Irish, English hymns and ballads

American music hall songs

Europe ▸ brass band marches French, Spanish, Italian songs

Europe's newly discovered folk dances inspired gay waltzes, *mazurkas*, *polkas*. These filled 19th century New York, Paris and London ballrooms. But by 1900 the jerky negro rhythms of the Cakewalk were challenging the smoothly gliding waltz. Dances derived from "savage" Africa were to swamp the dance halls of the Western world.

How did this happen? It began when West African slaves, shipped to North America, brought with them tribal songs and dances. To a negro, dance and music were still half-magic arts. He sang and danced for each event in life.

Work songs eased his toil in cotton fields. There, perhaps, a negro first heard Western music: a Christian preacher's hymns. Hymn tunes were European tunes or written by European settlers. Ignorant of the "rules" of Western music, negroes sang hymns to native rhythms, inventing spirituals.

When slaves gained freedom, negroes performed native dances and music in New Orleans' Congo Square. New Orleans' negroes also copied white men's brass bands. In carnival parades they played old army instruments, bought cheaply after the Civil War. But they played white men's tunes to lively, improvised, negro rhythms.

African dance and music-making played too great a part on every occasion in negro life for Western arts to drive them out. Even after a solemn funeral a negro band gaily struck up "Oh Didn't He Ramble," while mourners jigged and strutted home.

In New Orleans people of many nations met. Negro musicians borrowed Irish, Scottish, French, Italian, Spanish tunes, but mingled them with negro rhythms and improvised jazz melodies. A French *quadrille*, jazzed, became the famous "Tiger Rag." Arts of Africa and Europe have become American.

Negro rhythms, soon popular with white musicians, changed white dances. The first "negro" dance may have been capered beside a New Orleans jazz brass band. It was not long before the lively, jerky, unexpected movements of strangely-named dances spread to New York, Paris and London. Suddenly they made the waltz seem watery and worn out.

Western social dancing had changed again to keep pace with a changing Western world. Aristocratic rule, age-old ways of life had given way to democratic government, new machines. As life's tempo speeded up, the Cakewalk, Bunny Hug, Grizzly Bear, Black Bottom gave young Westerners the thrills they sought and failed to find in waltz or *polka*.

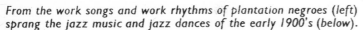

From the work songs and work rhythms of plantation negroes (left) sprang the jazz music and jazz dances of the early 1900's (below).

Dances spread across the world. Indian gestures appear in a Spanish dance (middle right). Music from Spain and rhythm from Africa (below right) reached America through settlement and slavery. New World negroes learned the European waltz (middle left). New World whites later danced to negro-derived rhythms (above and below, left). Both New and Old World dances meet in modern Europe (above right).

The story of social dance is a story of movement in time and space. Always as they move, dances take with them something of the land they come from.

The history of dancing is almost all unwritten. Thus we often have to read between the dancer's living movements to guess how they became like that.

The *jota* of Spanish Aragon is said to have been invented by an exiled Moorish poet. But in such stories there is often more than meets the eye. Some Spanish dances have gestures strange to other European dances. We know that gypsies, numerous in Spain, may have brought with them Indian gesture dances when they spread to Europe many centuries ago. We know that Africa's Arab Moors invaded Dark Age Spain and brought their own arts with them. For all we know, dance movements born in Europe, Africa and Asia meet in the Spanish *jota*.

The names of many dances hint at the lands that bred them: the *polonaise* from Poland, the *allemande* from Allemagne (Germany), the now forgotten *canary* from the Canary Islands.

Old dances sailed with the first Spaniards to colonize the New World. Mexican Aztec's dances mixed with the colonists and sailed back to Spain. In this way new dances, the *chaconne* and *sarabande*, were brought to Europe. But in 1583 a law decreed 200 lashes and six years as a galley slave for any Spaniard who sang the *sarabande's* songs. The vigorous *chaconne* and *sarabande*, like the Charleston 300 years later, shocked people of refined ways of life.

Dances went from the New World to the Old, from Old to New. European courtly dances fused with Amerindian pantomime. African rhythms mingled with Spanish song and dance. From such mixtures have evolved the Cuban *rumba*, Brazil's *maxixe*, Chile's *cueca*, Argentina's *tango*.

Thus the most "modern" dance is often one of the world's most ancient, transplanted direct from steaming jungle to city dance hall. As better transport has opened up the world, so-called savage arts have brought fresh life to Western arts: to painting, sculpture, social dance and ballet.

In recent years, the age-old arts of savage Africa (above) gave inspiration to the Western world's most modern paintings (below).

59

Banquets and Ballet

60

A circus acrobat and ballet dancer perform very different dances. But both entertain an audience. Without an audience neither would dance at all.

As we have seen, dancing as an entertainment flourishes only where people can afford time and money to watch performers more skilled and graceful than themselves. When Rome's civilization broke up, entertainment dances nearly died out. For almost uncharted centuries, the only dancing entertainers had to travel far, from one isolated castle to the next, between small, widely scattered villages.

A joculator (juggler-acrobat) had to be several entertainers rolled in one. He sang, he played the harp, he juggled, danced and tumbled. Some joculators even taught tame bears to dance and mimic human actions, walking upright like a man.

Partly because he was always on the move, partly because he was not rich, the joculator had to travel light. He impressed less by graceful dances in lavish costumes than by acrobatic movements of his body: leaping, tumbling, turning somersaults.

We read of one such dancer who amazed his audience with "goings, turnings, tumblings, castings, hops, jumps, leaps, skips, springs, gambauds, somersaults, capretings, and flights, forward, backward, sideways, downward, upward, and with sundry windings, gyrings and circumflections."

As trade increased and towns grew larger, dancer-acrobats entertained the medieval townsfolk. In time,

In medieval Europe, the acrobatic dancers who performed at nobles' castle banquets also entertained the commoners at country fairs.

performers joined into little troupes. Most famous of these entertainers played in Italy's *commedia dell' arte*: the mimic actor-dancers whose skill perhaps went back to the silent mimed dances of ancient Rome. The *commedia dell' arte* invented Columbine and Harlequin and other characters and costumes which we see in circus acts today. Both in circus rings and music halls we witness acrobatic dancing of the sort which entertained both castle barons and country peasants almost 1,000 years ago.

The history of popular acrobatic dancing is almost all unwritten. But the story of ballet is complete. From the chroniclers of bygone courts to the dance-designer choreographers of the present day, people have sketched its scenes, described its steps. For ballet, unlike acrobatic dance, developed in an atmosphere of learning. Unlike acrobatic dance, ballet evolved in princely courts alone.

BALLI DI SFESSANIA
·di Jacomo Callot·

Left: 17th century engravings show Italy's commedia dell' arte: the bands of miming actor-dancers who performed in city squares.

Royal processions such as this, which welcomed an Italian prince to Florence, foreshadowed the court displays which led to ballet.

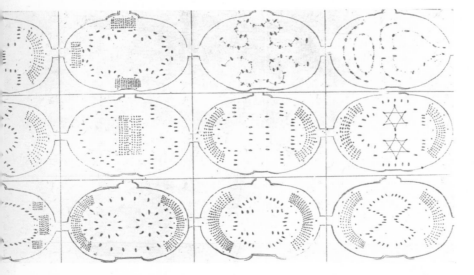

Above: Each pageant was a pattern made up of many performers. Below: Each performer's splendid tunic was paid for by a prince.

Acrobatic dancing could flourish in any village square. The spectacles that led to ballet could not. They were lavish entertainments paid for by Italian merchant princes' wealth. Their wealth, won from trade, also paid for splendid works of art and helped to create the Renaissance, Italy's rebirth of classic Graeco-Roman art and learning.

Partly as patrons of art, partly to display their wealth, Medici princes paid for splendid open-air processions. Magnificently decorated floats and costumed courtiers marched in imitation of a Roman general's triumphal parade.

At indoor banquets *entremets* became the fashion: courtiers would dance in, carrying the loaded plates. The French word *entremet* meaning "sweet course" comes from this. In 1489, a famous banquet celebrated the marriage of the Duke of Milan to Isabella of Aragon. Dancing servers, disguised as Greek gods, introduced each of its many courses.

The fame of this banquet spread. In England, court *masques* became the fashion: displays where dance, poetry, music, scenes delighted the senses. In Italy, *mascarades* led to opera. In France, dance displays in time became classic ballet, which gains its name from Italy's *balletti*: court dance displays.

Some date the birth of ballet from 1581. In France that year a splendid spectacle celebrated the be-

trothal of the Duc de Joyeuse to Margaret of Lorraine. Baldassarino Belgiojoso, an Italian violinist, designed this "Ballet Comique de la Reine" which re-enacted the ancient Greek legend of Ulysses who, aided by the gods, escaped the witch, Circe. Ten thousand guests saw the performance. It cost more than three million francs.

Early ballets differed greatly from the art we know today. Scenery stood dispersed throughout a ballroom hall. Painted with a background picture, a large cloth hung from one end. Before it stood a wood and canvas castle. Before that might be a bed of flowers. Grottoes concealed musicians. Painted cloth "clouds" hung from the ceiling. From them, "gods" and "goddesses" descended to the earth below where candles, masked by tinted glass, produced unearthly light. Dancers entered through vaults of greenery.

Courtiers both danced and planned these ballets. Courtiers also made up most of the audience which sat on stands or galleries raised all round the hall. The audience looked down on dancers from all sides. Early ballets were the interweaving patterns made up of stately figures, sumptuously dressed. Probably the courtier-dancers barely raised their legs above the ground. Such a spectacle was more like a display of military countermarching seen from a stadium, than a ballet as we see it from theatre stalls today.

Figure patterns created by 8,000 people for a modern Czechoslovak gym display remind us of some courtly ballet on gigantic scale.

Performed and drawn in 17th century Florence, "The Liberation of Tirreno" shows a court ballet as the spectators must have seen it.

Left: Ballet grew up at Versailles, thanks to the patronage and dancing of Louis XIV, pictured in the ballet costume of the Sun.

Before classic ballet had grown up in France, Cardinal Mazarin tried to make Italian opera a French courtly fashion. A witness of one such opera wrote: "This comedy lasted over six hours. It was beautiful to see once, so striking were the changes of scenery; but the sheer length of it was boring, although no one dared show it, and even those who did not understand Italian pretended to enjoy it."

The young king Louis XIV was as bored as his subjects. His interest lay in dancing more than song. When only 13, Louis had danced in the ballet called "Cassandre." Of course the King always took the leading part when he performed.

Through Louis' efforts, ballet, not opera, grew up at the Versailles Court. But French ballet owed much to the Italian Lully. He was composer, dancer, choreographer and accomplished courtier. Largely thanks to him, ballet became more than just dancing for its own sake. With the poet Benserade and the dancing master Beauchamp, Lully helped to make a ballet tell a story through its steps and gestures.

With the famous playwright Molière, he produced plays like "Le Bourgeois Gentilhomme" including dancing and drama. "Let us join all three," wrote Molière (meaning dancing, comedy and music). He aimed to do what Greece had done, what the Chinese drama had always aimed at, what we mistakenly hail as novelty in musicals like "Oklahoma."

In 1636 Cardinal Richelieu built the first French theatre. Soon, plays moved from court to stage. Theatres offered more to dance as well as drama. For instance, stage designers could conceal canvas clouds' mechanical workings more easily behind a proscenium arch than on a ballroom ceiling.

Adorned with priceless paintings, Versailles' spacious "Galerie des Glaces" reflects the leisured elegance of Louis XIV's court.

Ballet went from court ballroom to theatre where audiences, seated below the stage, clearly saw each dancer's separate movements.

The complex step-pattern of the bourrée – one of several courtly social dances which grew too hard for all but experts to perform.

On a raised stage, ballet became quite different. Performers now all faced one way toward the audience. The audience could see more clearly the movements of their legs, arms and bodies.

In time ballet became less a stately gliding of many figures, more the expert, livelier steps and gestures of solo dancers. Skilful solo dancers inspired dancing masters to devise more complex patterns. Social dances like the minuet and *bourrée* became a spectacle which only trained artists could perform.

Thus ballet ceased to be the leisure-hour amusement of courtier dancers. It became the lifetime's study of an expert paid to dance. The proscenium arch separating an audience from the dancers on a stage helped to increase the gap which separated those who do from those who watch – a gap as wide today as it has ever been.

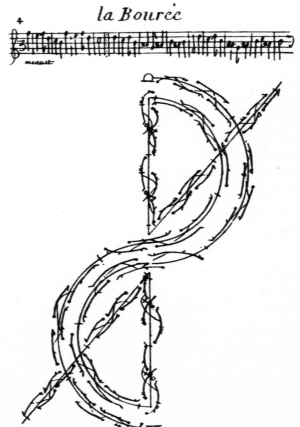

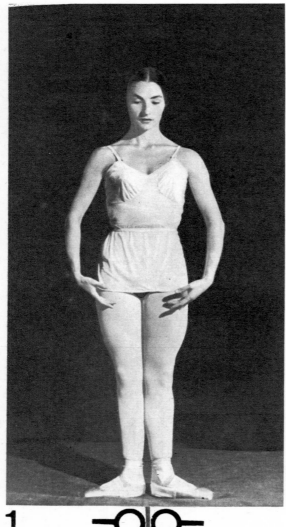

Part of an example of Feuillet's ballet shorthand shows straight line marking the dancer's path around the room. Bars which cut the dancer's path correspond to bars of music. Letters mark the steps and notes performed together.

A slide.
A rise.
A sink.
Bar ends.
No steps within first bar.
Left foot.
Right foot.
The dancer begins here.

In 1661 King Louis XIV founded *l'Académie Royale de la Danse*, made up of 13 ballet masters with Beauchamp at their head. A room was set aside for them at the Louvre Palace but the dancers preferred the homely comfort of a tavern, *l'Epée de Bois*. There, they devised rules for the correct steps for ballet, based on the five "positions."

These five positions of the feet were planned to give balance to any position of the body. They were both a starting and an ending point for any ballet dance. Today, with minor changes, they are still the basis of all classical ballet.

Many of the old dances and all the old ballets have been forgotten. No way of writing down and thus preserving steps had been invented. Past efforts at dance notation had been incomplete. Even today no world-wide system is in use, as there is for music. But in 1701 a new notation appeared. Raoul Feuillet's *Chorégraphie*, or "the art of how to write down a dance," rapidly grew popular.

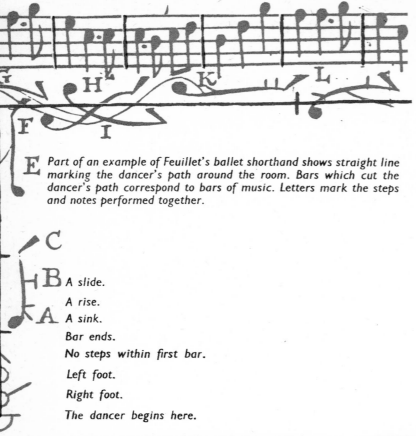

1

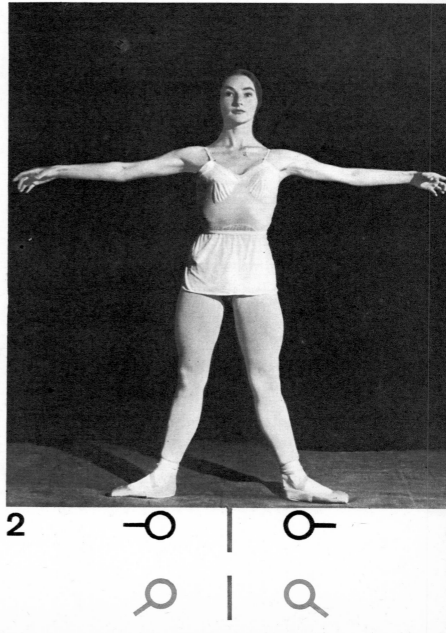

2

Feuillet's system showed the dancer's movements from above. A straight line marked the dancer's path. Symbols placed by and on the line stood for his steps. Bars at intervals across the line marked off the steps he was to dance within one bar of music. The music itself stood printed above the dance notation. This system both helped to teach new steps and to hand on old ones. For many years, ballet teachers made use of Feuillet's invention.

Greatest of all the teachers was probably Jean Georges Noverre (1727-1810), the father of modern ballet. Influenced by the great English actor David Garrick, he was the first choreographer to use the plots of great plays as ballet stories.

Today ballet teachers still prize Noverre's famous *Lettres sur la Danse et les Ballets*. He wrote that steps must be skilful but that skill displayed for its own sake is bad. Dancers should make steps and gestures reveal the feelings of the characters they represent. Even "the hands of a capable dancer must be able to speak; if his face is not expressive, if his eyes are not eloquent, then everything is without meaning." Noverre's letters also wisely show that not all music can be danced to, not all stories can be told in mime.

In Italy in 1797 was born the teacher who perfected classic ballet. When only 17, Carlo Blasis wrote a book to bring Noverre's teachings "up to date." He showed that human movements depend upon the law of gravity and how our bodies are made.

He wrote: "A person that carries a burthen placed out of the central line of his body, must necessarily add, from his own weight, a balance sufficient to counterpoise it on the opposite side . . ." To dance well, one must walk gracefully. "Your steps should be no longer than the length of one of your feet."

But Carlo Blasis' aim was not to make a ballet dance a list of steps to copy. He suggested that dancers should make up practice steps themselves to well-known airs. Like Noverre, he knew that skilful repetition of ballet steps did not make a ballerina.

The five positions of legs and arms. Diagrams: modern turn out of feet (black) gives better balance and mobility than old (terra cotta).

3   4   5

Above: 19th century costumes give grace and freedom of movement.
Below: Ornate 18th century costumes restrained dancers' steps.

Habit d'Architecte

Ia - le Pautre Sculp.

In 1650 the ballerina was unknown. Boys played all female parts. But by 1850, male ballet dancers themselves were almost rare. How did this happen?

In 1681 women first appeared, in a ballet called "Le Triomphe de l'Amour." Famous ballerinas soon appeared: the rivals Marie Sallé and Marie Camargo. In the century that followed, men and women only played the stately parts of Greek and Roman gods and goddesses. But, by 1800, as we have seen, Europe's ways of life and tastes in art were changing.

Ballet began to take its stories more from the romantic legends of northern lakes and forests, less from the classic myths of southern Europe. Théophile Gautier, poet and inspirer of ballet wrote: "Gone are the twelve gold and marble dwellings of the Olympians, now all that is ordered from the scene painters are the romantic forests and the valleys lit by the beautiful German moonlight of the ballads of Henri Heine." Both scenes and characters changed.

Greek and Roman gods gave way to *wilis*, sylphs and fairies of northern lands. Graceful dancers, poised as if in flight, or skimming over water, took their parts. Marie Taglioni gained fame as *La Sylphide*, a frail heroine from the spirit world who could "glide over flowers without bending them."

Taglioni was a "spiritual" dancer. Her great rival, Fanny Elssler, drew strength and inspiration from the earth beneath her feet. Unsuited to Taglioni's fairy roles, she excelled in dramatic dances demanding power as well as skill.

Shortening dress to suit her lively style of dance, Marie Anne de Cupis de Camargo (1710-70) helped to create ballet as we know it.

Above: Marie Taglioni (1804-84) gained her fame in fairy roles. Below: Fanny Elssler (1810-84) became Taglioni's greatest rival.

Both Elssler and Taglioni owed their popularity to steps no dancer could have done a century before. Then, ballerinas, wearing masks and carrying cupids' bows or garlands, were encumbered by wide, heavy skirts and high-heeled shoes.

La Camargo was the first to raise her skirt several inches and to remove her heels. Lighter skirts led to the *tutu* which ballet dancers still wear in "Swan Lake," "Giselle," "The Sleeping Beauty" and other classic ballets. Flat ballet shoes led to ballet slippers with "blocked" toes which help a ballerina stand on her points to imitate a flying fairy. Freer clothes helped to create freer, leaping dances. Leaping dances led to fresh experiments in writing down a dance to show it from the side, not from above.

As freer costumes helped make Elssler and Taglioni roles more famous, male dancers' roles grew ever less important. Women *en travesti* (in disguise) took their parts. They even danced both parts of a *pas de deux*, a love duet, ridiculous without the contrast of a man's and woman's movements.

Ballerinas became stars, the idols of their devoted audience. Ambassadors, ministers, noblemen and bankers met these dancers in the *foyer de la danse* of the Paris Opéra and vied to give them splendid gifts.

Star ballerinas often insisted on displaying their most brilliant steps, although these might be unsuited to the ballet into which they had to fit. Such acrobatic dancing may have gained fame for the ballerina, but it did nothing for the art of ballet.

Lively dances like the cachuca (made famous by Elssler) inspired Zorn's dance shorthand designed to show movements from the side.

Charles Beauchamp (1636-1705)

Louis Pécour (1655-1729)

Louis Dupré (1697-1774)

Jean Georges Noverre (1727-1810)

Dauberval (1742-1806)

Carlo Blasis (1797-1878)

Giovanni Lepri (portrait about 1857)

Enrico Cecchetti (1850-1928)

Ninette de Valois (1898-   )

70

Left: Teachers, in unbroken line from Beauchamp to the present day, created classic ballet. Above: By 1890, all classic ballet steps had been invented. Thus Stepanov, a Russian dancer, could devise this dance shorthand. Its symbols, learned like notes of music, stood for classic ballet movements. Upper example shows grands battements, lower shows pas jetés. Below: Bored by ballerinas brilliantly performing classic steps, 19th century cartoonists compared their whirlings with the spinning of a wooden top.

APOCALYPSE DU BALLET.
Dessin de Grandville.

We have seen how both Italian courts and French theatres, ballet dancers and ballet masters made classic ballet dancing what it is today.

We can trace the ballet story in an unbroken line, through the people who have taught it, from Beauchamp three centuries ago, to George Balanchine, Serge Lifar and Ninette de Valois at the present day.

Almost all the teachers' names reveal they came from Italy or France, the lands that saw the birth of ballet. Yet today ballet has gained world-wide fame.

Had classic ballet remained a thing of Italy and France, this might never have happened. It came to pass because French and Italian ballet teachers and ballet companies went to Russia.

In 1893 Italy's Pierrina Legnani astonished St. Petersburg audiences by spinning on one point to turn 32 *fouettés* non-stop. But Russian dancers had already fused Western dances with their own.

During the reign of Catherine the Great, well before 1800, serf dancers entertained at court. Later, Russia's Imperial Ballet drew many of its members from companies of dancing serfs. Fifty years before all other peasants gained their freedom, serf dancers were granted theirs.

Russian ballet was perfected by a Frenchman Petipa, a Swede Johannsen, an Italian Cecchetti. But Russian ballet had vitality, born of peasant dances, which Western ballet, far from its origins, lacked.

By 1900, Russian dancers had gained world-wide fame. Kchessinska, Trefilova, Preobrajenska, Pavlova, Karsavina became household names. The fame of Russian ballet helped to inspire the birth of ballet companies in other lands.

Yet in 1905 an American went to Russia "to show that classic ballet was all wrong." Isadora Duncan said that dancing should not be the repetition of ready-made steps. It should be free. It should express the dancer's inner feelings. She had no orthodox dance technique. Barefoot, in flowing draperies, she danced as her feelings led her, to music of great composers. Thus, she thought, the Greeks had danced 2,000 years before.

Russia's Michael Fokine defended ballet. He said that "man should and could be expressive from head to foot." Yet he also said the greatest dancer must play his part as one member of a group – the ballet company. The company itself is but one quarter of a ballet. For ballet is not the same as ballet dancing. It is music, dancing, drama, painting: four equal partners making up one whole.

Bored by classic ballet, inspired by Greek sculpture (above), Isadora Duncan (below) believed that we should dance as feelings prompt us (right), not to ready-made steps laid down by experts in the art of ballet.

Theatre-box party, caricatured by Cocteau who provided themes for several "Ballets Russes," shows the impresario Diaghilev (right).

1915 photo shows members of Diaghilev's team. Left-right: Massine (dancer-choreographer), Goncharova (designer), Larionov (designer-producer, above), Stravinsky (composer, below), Bakst (designer).

A Ballet is Born

Serge Diaghilev, a Russian impresario – the term is inadequate to express his role – put into practice Fokine's ideas. He knew that artists, composers, poets, dancers must all combine to make a ballet a great work of art.

Diaghilev built up such a team and, with his help, great painters, composers, dancers, poets united for one purpose for the first time since the days of court *balletti* and the age of Molière.

Vaslav Nijinsky, a Pole, the son of dancers, brought new life to the roles of men in ballet. He was to become the world's most famous male dancer. Léon Bakst created scenes and costumes of pagan Eastern splendor, far different from the romantic forest scenes and white tarlatan *tutus* which had ruled the stage so long. Igor Stravinsky wrote music which seemed strangely harsh and full of action after Chopin's music in "Les Sylphides." Writers and choreographers suggested new themes: an Arabian Nights story, a Greek faun's afternoon, a pagan springtime rite – refreshing changes from the fairy-witch-and-hero tales of romantic ballet, performed with little alteration during 70 years.

With his Ballets Russes, Diaghilev toured western Europe, then the United States. Audiences went wild with excitement at the virile, leaping Polovtsian dances from "Prince Igor," leaps which hinted at the very origins of tribal war dance. Thrilled by Bakst's "Schéhérazade" designs, the whole of Paris went oriental. People held Arabian Nights balls, fashions changed almost overnight, indoor decorations were transformed.

Thanks largely to Diaghilev, this century has seen many experiments: new steps, new ways of writing dances down, new music, themes and stage designs.

But whether new or old, no two ballets are put together in the same way. Sometimes a story inspires a choreographer, sometimes a dancer inspires a piece of music. Diaghilev himself supplied the spark that started several ballets. But without his team no ballets would have been completed.

Someone must invent the ballet theme, but someone must plan the ballet's steps, someone must dance them, someone must write the music, someone must design the décor. In this chapter we shall see something of the many parts that go to make up ballet.

Leon Bakst's designs for "Schéhérazade" brought vivid Eastern hues to Western ballet, where dim forest scenery had long prevailed.

Nijinsky's "l'Après Midi d'un Faune" startled ballet fans with its turned-in steps, strange costumes and a male dancer in the lead.

On points, like a European "sylphide," but in brilliant scarlet costume, a ballerina plays the "firebird" of a Russian legend.

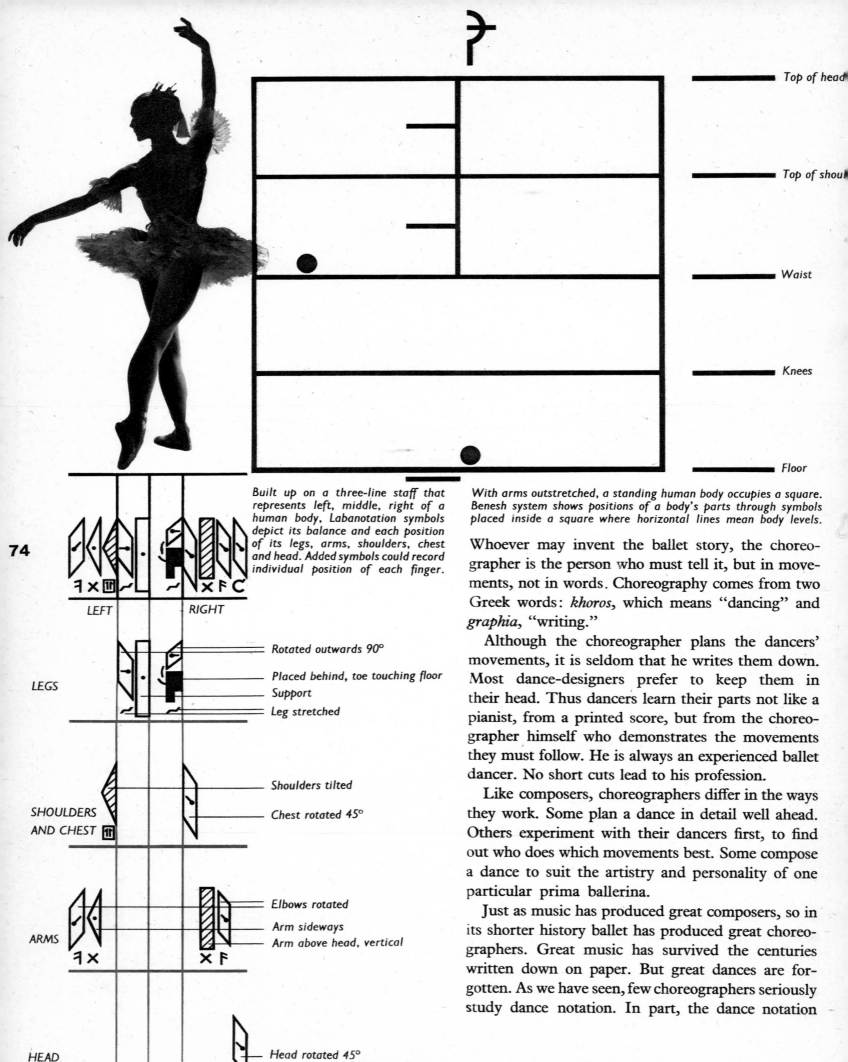

Top of head

Top of shoul

Waist

Knees

Floor

Built up on a three-line staff that represents left, middle, right of a human body, Labanotation symbols depict its balance and each position of its legs, arms, shoulders, chest and head. Added symbols could record individual position of each finger.

LEFT   RIGHT

LEGS

Rotated outwards 90°

Placed behind, toe touching floor
Support
Leg stretched

SHOULDERS
AND CHEST

Shoulders tilted

Chest rotated 45°

ARMS

Elbows rotated

Arm sideways
Arm above head, vertical

HEAD

Head rotated 45°

With arms outstretched, a standing human body occupies a square. Benesh system shows positions of a body's parts through symbols placed inside a square where horizontal lines mean body levels.

Whoever may invent the ballet story, the choreographer is the person who must tell it, but in movements, not in words. Choreography comes from two Greek words: *khoros*, which means "dancing" and *graphia*, "writing."

Although the choreographer plans the dancers' movements, it is seldom that he writes them down. Most dance-designers prefer to keep them in their head. Thus dancers learn their parts not like a pianist, from a printed score, but from the choreographer himself who demonstrates the movements they must follow. He is always an experienced ballet dancer. No short cuts lead to his profession.

Like composers, choreographers differ in the ways they work. Some plan a dance in detail well ahead. Others experiment with their dancers first, to find out who does which movements best. Some compose a dance to suit the artistry and personality of one particular prima ballerina.

Just as music has produced great composers, so in its shorter history ballet has produced great choreographers. Great music has survived the centuries written down on paper. But great dances are forgotten. As we have seen, few choreographers seriously study dance notation. In part, the dance notation

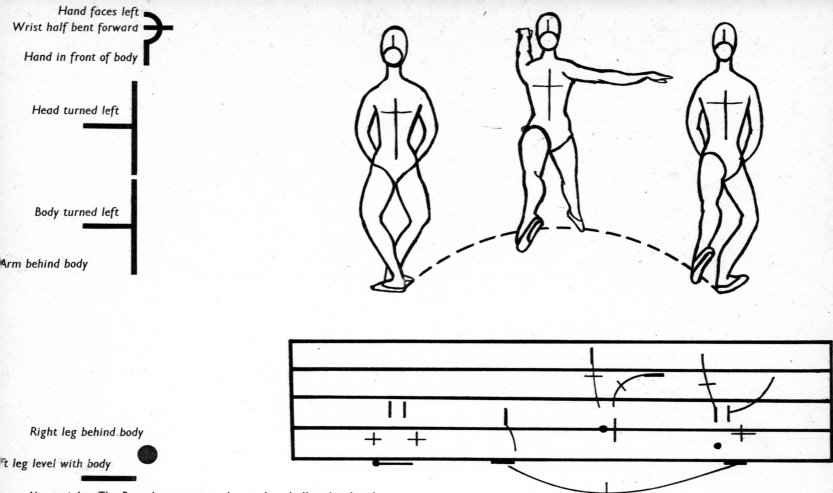

Hand faces left
Wrist half bent forward
Hand in front of body

Head turned left

Body turned left

Arm behind body

Right leg behind body
t leg level with body

Above right: The Benesh system can be used as ballet shorthand. In a grand jeté leap, movement lines show path of hands and feet.

systems themselves have been to blame for this. All those invented in the past have had their faults.

Today, two new ways of writing dance-movements may help to solve this problem for the future. Perhaps most useful to a choreographer, the Benesh system is a ballet shorthand. A five-line stave within a square shows the levels of a standing dancer's head, shoulders, waist, knees, feet. Symbols placed against these lines indicate each movement which the dancer makes. A dot means "behind the body," a horizontal dash "level with the body," a vertical dash "in front of the body." Thus in the example on page 74, a dot placed on the line for "waist" but to the left of the square shows the dancer's left arm, held at waist-level behind the body.

Slower to write, more difficult to learn, but some claim more precise, Labanotation takes its name from Rudolf Laban, its inventor. It claims to represent every possible movement of the human body, from a dancer's *pirouette* to the twitching of her little toe. Its symbols can show whether a movement is a punch, press, dab, glide, slash, wring, flick or float. Labanotation can show the movements of factory worker, swimmer, acrobat or ballerina with equal ease and detailed accuracy.

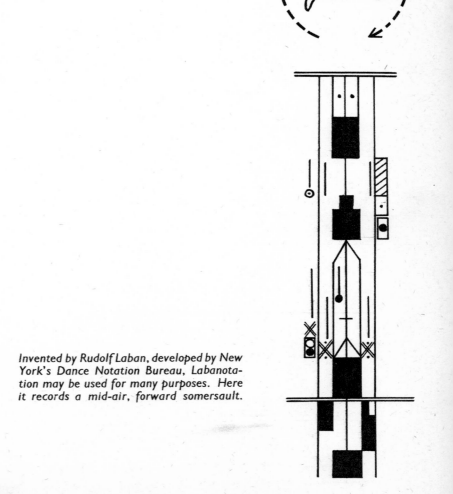

Invented by Rudolf Laban, developed by New York's Dance Notation Bureau, Labanotation may be used for many purposes. Here it records a mid-air, forward somersault.

Daily practice and woman's supple limbs combine to create the graceful movements of the ballerina as we see her on the stage.

Ballet is one-fourth drama. Thus ballet dancers are also actors, expressing drama through their dance. But they must learn how to dance before they can hope to make a dance dramatic.

Would-be dancers should start learning at an early age. Girls begin between the ages of 10 and 11, boys a little later. St.-Léon, a violinist in the Paris Opéra, did not begin to learn until he was 20. Then he fell in love with a ballerina and wanted to join her on the stage. St.-Léon became a fine dancer but he remains an exception to the general rule.

Fashions in shapes of ballet dancers change. Two centuries ago engravings showed them short and plump. To Théophile Gautier the thin dancer was a criminal! Today young dancers must always take the risk that they may grow either too heavy or too tall.

Yet a modern dancer's training is little altered from the time of Carlo Blasis. An audition that includes a medical examination first decides whether a pupil is fit enough to take up ballet as a career. But fitness is not enough. A dancer must have both a sense of rhythm and a true sense of music.

In the simplest costumes, revealing every faulty movement, boys and girls practise at a bar fixed waist-high along a wall. One or two hours daily at the bar helps to make supple limbs.

Girls and boys are made differently. Ballerinas should be light and graceful, best at supple, flexible movements of their limbs. Male dancers must be strong, prepared to lift a ballerina effortlessly to shoulder height, to leap with the vitality of a savage. Yet, like a ballerina, they must land with grace.

Graceful movement is also rhythmic movement. Joe Louis was a graceful boxer. Boxing needs rhythmic grace as much as ballet. Yet many boys wrongly think it "cissy" for a man to be a dancer. Thus fewer boys than girls take up ballet and those who do must often learn in class with girls. Unconsciously they sometimes copy women's movements. This is wrong, for ballet should stress the difference between the ballerina and her partner.

Learning ballet is more than learning to be a professional dancer. Carefully taught, its disciplined movements can help to remedy defects. At least two famous ballerinas began to learn after attacks of polio. Another started as a cure for knock-knees. The quick co-ordination of mind and limb required to put together steps are as valuable as any other training. Dancing as education, understood by the Greeks, today is coming to the fore again.

With limbs less supple, but more powerful than a woman's, a male dancer's virile leaps are every bit as graceful as a ballerina's.

Degas' bronze statuette depicts a would-be ballerina who started training at an early age. Years of constant practice lie behind the seeming ease with which a ballet dancer smoothly moves across a stage. For she must master every muscle in her body as a concert pianist must command control of every note upon the keyboard.

Feminine suppleness, masculine strength blend together perfectly in such scenes as this, taken from the famous "Swan Lake" ballet.

Left: A grand jeté of the 17th century
Below: A grand jeté from a recent ballet

78

Left: A cabriol leap from classic ballet
Below: Free leaping in a modern musical

17th century experiments led to classic ballet's recognized steps.
20th century experiments create fresh, unnamed, freer movements.

Choreographers plan a ballet dance; dancers dramatize it through their movements. Just as separate parts, united, form the whole ballet, separate movements, joined together, create the ballet dance.

Already we have seen that there are five positions of the feet: positions to give a dancer balance at the start and finish of each movement. The five positions of a dancer's arms are also designed for grace and balance. Even a single arm and the dancer's head have five positions allotted to them.

About 100 miming gestures help to dramatize a ballet. Thus right hand placed on heart means "I love you." Most ballet mime is simple; its gestures are far fewer than the Hindu *mudras*.

Although ballet movements are often known as *pas* or steps, arms, head, legs should all combine to create one graceful movement.

Classic ballet contains seven basic sorts of movement: *plier* (to bend), *étendre* (to stretch), *relever* (to raise), *glisser* (to glide), *sauter* (to jump), *élancer* (to dart), *tourner* (to turn). These are the simplest. On these, more complex movements are built up; movements like the *entrechat*, a leap in which the dancer crosses legs several times in mid-air; the triple *tour en l'air*, three turns in the air without touching the ground; the *pirouette*, a turning movement of the body, often on the points alone. A *pirouette* may finish in a graceful *arabesque* or in an *attitude*, a position said to have been developed by Carlo Blasis, inspired by a statue of the god Mercury.

A sequence of positions, movements, *attitudes*, makes up an *enchaînement*. Linked *enchaînements* form a *variation*. *Variations* for the leading dancers, with movements for the *corps de ballet*, with music and scenery, make up the whole performance.

When ballet grew up, in the French Court, French was the international language, just as Latin was once the language common to all learned men. Today French terms remain in ballet as Latin names still scientifically describe plants and animals.

Today, in classic ballet, dancers learn the same steps taught 100 years ago. But a good ballerina does not aim to dance them more cleverly than the great dancers of the past. She has a feeling for the rhythm of the music to which she dances. Through her fixed pattern of steps she tries to interpret the music's mood. But she must also be an actress. Like an actress in a play she brings to her ready-written part the way in which she sees it. Rarely do two actors or two dancers perform one piece alike.

A photographic "still" freezes in motion grand battement (*above right*) and arabesque (*below right*). Multiple exposure of film (*above and below left*) shows both positions are but moments in a chain of separate movements, flowing smoothly into one another.

"Giselle," most popular of ballets, is one of the most difficult to act. At first its heroine, a carefree village girl, is gay and laughing. Betrayed by her lover, she goes mad. In unco-ordinated stumbling steps, she fumbles where before she danced so gracefully. Then she becomes a spirit, unhappy because she loves a mortal and would not drag him to his death at the bidding of her cruel Queen. The ballerina has to be both a spiritual Taglioni and an earthy Elssler.

The romantic costume and make-up help to establish the character both for the dancer and the audience. Tamara Karsavina has written of how the painting of the eyebrows in front of her dressing table mirror gave her the clue to the character of the cruel Georgian Queen Thamar. The fringed beard helps Michael Somes in his remarkable interpretation of Creon in "Antigone." The important thing to realize is that costume and make-up are useless unless they become a part of the personality and physique of the dancer.

Make-up and costume help to transform an everyday person from the everyday world of grimy city life into a god, a dragon, or a bird which flies or flutters inside a magic world lit, not by the sun, but by the enchanting glow of many-hued spotlights.

Yet the designer who brings about this miracle must remain very much down-to-earth. He must know what materials best make a dragon or a god, how they will look in the light of day and how theatre lighting will change their hues and textures. His costumes must help, not hinder, dancers' movements. A designer must not give a ballerina feathers which tickle her partner's nose to make him sneeze in their *pas de deux*, often the highlight of a ballet.

The stage-designer must always bear in mind that ballet is a drama of movement. His décor must not excite us more than the dancers' steps and gestures. From every scene on earth and in the designer's fertile mind, he may choose only what is vital to help tell the ballet story or to set its mood.

In "Giselle" we simply see a village and a forest glade. On the stage, neither ever has all the details of a real-life village or forest glade. The designer's art lies in his selective eye, in suggesting through simple designs the place, the atmosphere in which a ballet story is supposed to happen.

So, too, with "abstract" ballets like "Symphonic Variations," which do not tell a tale. The simplest lines and colors may echo in pictures the music's mood, to make a perfect setting for the dance.

Costumes transform 20th century dancers into the clowning, miming actor-dancers of 17th century Italian commedia dell' arte.

Subtle additions to the ballet dancer's basic costume can suggest the character he represents: here the famous "Spectre de la Rose."

In every country costume plays a part in dance and drama. A giant costume for several people creates this Chinese carnival dragon.

Scenery helps to tell a story or create a mood. Here it reflects the rhythms of "Symphonic Variations," ballet built round music.

Left: An elaborately costumed dancing master in Louis XIV's age of stately ballet. Middle: Wilis pursue their human victim in "Giselle," romantic ballet of a century ago. Right: In 1900 modern industry inspired this spectacle. Ballerinas on points brandished electric bulbs.

In nearly four centuries, ballet has seen many changes – from Roman gods to German fairies, from classic *tutus* to modern tights, from feet turned out as taught by Carlo Blasis to feet turned in as danced by Nijinsky in "l'Après Midi d'un Faune," from the sedate dignity of the "Ballet Comique de la Reine" to the free leaping of dancers in modern ballets.

Ballet has changed, and with it, ballet audiences. Once the privileges which went with noble birth were needed before one could witness a select court performance. Today anyone can see the world's greatest prima ballerina simply by buying a ticket.

Unfortunately ballerinas are all that many people do pay to see. And many in each audience still think the greatest dancer is the one who can do the most *fouettés* non-stop. Others go only to hear the music, to follow the story or to see so-and-so's latest stage design. To anyone who reads this book, ballet should now mean more than any one of the arts of dancing, painting, drama, music as they appear in ballet.

Outside the ballet each one of these is an art in itself. We need all our attention on the music of a Bach fugue to enjoy it. Even were it possible for a dancer to dance to it she would more likely distract than delight us. A Rembrandt painting as a ballet backcloth also would not work.

But ballet music, ballet dancing, ballet stage design, a ballet theme – each is designed to be one quarter of a whole. Each one of these ingredients must be mixed to conjure up the magic that is ballet.

Experiments in modern dance cast off the rules of classic ballet. Above: Free leaping to the music of a single drum in a drama without scenery.
Below: Dancers of the "Ballets Jooss," in attitudes and costumes never seen in any classic ballet, mimic statesmen at a conference.

Mambo and Musical

In a Spanish dance, bottles of perfumed water smashed ceremonially on a church roof hint at an ancient rain-making ritual. But the dancers have long forgotten the ritual meaning of this act. Today, in the civilized world, we no longer dance for rain. We spray clouds with dry ice from a plane.

Old Stone Age people probably danced only to make things happen. Today, machines replace magic dances, but civilized peoples need social dances and dances of entertainment as much as ever.

As man's control over his environment increased, he built more and more factories – factories sited near cities. Growing 19th century factories drew ever more people from the country to the city to find work. Today, city populations are bigger than ever before. New York, London, Tokyo each have about 10 million inhabitants.

These huge city populations need places where people can meet and make friends, somewhere where a conversation is not two minutes' gossip snatched on an escalator in the daily rush-hour. Ballrooms and dance halls help to satisfy this social need. In city dance halls thousands meet in leisure hours.

In the medieval past a peasant's life was almost all work. A noble's life was almost all leisure. Today, all city dwellers earn their own living, yet all of us have far more leisure time than any medieval peasant. Thus, in a sense, each is both peasant and noble.

The man who gets greasy from head to foot oiling factory machines this morning may be immaculate in dinner jacket, waltzing around a palatial ballroom this evening. Or, dressed in jeans and T-shirt, he may prefer the lively, unsophisticated movements of a square dance. The choice is his.

Once all peasants danced peasant dances, all nobles trod courtly steps. Today, democracy has banished class divisions both of people and their dances. An English duke may rock 'n' roll in a night-club cellar and waltz at a royal ball without anyone raising an eyebrow in surprise. Your taste, not your class, determines whether the dance you prefer is inspired more by savages or dancing masters.

Your taste, not your class, determines the dance you watch. You may prefer chorus girls to the *corps de ballet*, music hall, born of fairground spectacles, to ballet, born at court. The choice is yours to make.

Far left: From the age when troubadours and minnesingers (pictured here) sang the praises of their lady and behaved according to the rules of etiquette laid down by "courtly love," nobles lived and danced without the freedom of a peasant. Near left: Though ways of life had changed a century ago, these people still always dressed and danced according to the "class" in which they lived.

Today the way you dress, behave and dance no longer reflects the "class" you live in. The man in top hat, white tie, tails (right) is Fred Astaire. He could be duke or cab driver equally as well. A square dance group (below) perhaps includes both office boys and millionaires, alike enjoying leisure hours in check shirts and jeans, the clothes that only peasants wore a century ago.

Bigger city populations have led to bigger dance halls. There, space helped modern waltz and flowing foxtrot flourish. But the crowded floors of many hotels led to "crush" dancing. Teenagers, impatient of "stand-still" dancing, created new dances, new "dance halls" in cellars and youth clubs.

Exciting dances do not suddenly appear ready-made. But modern dance inventors can freely dip into the storehouse of negro rhythm, adapting it to city life. In negro-inspired jive and jitterbug, bebop, rock 'n' roll, city teenagers have found what they wanted. Hip-swinging, knee-swaying, throwing their partner – here was all and more of the free vitality of the old *ländler*, once Europe's most lively dance.

Until 1770 the *ländler* was little known outside its native Austria. By 1820 the *ländler*-derived waltz had

In a teeming modern capital, a crowded dance hall (above) often provides the only place where teenage friends can meet (right).

swept the world. Today, through modern travel, new dances spread much faster. In 1912 Argentina's *tango* gained fame in Paris within a year. Mid-century rock 'n' roll swept first the United States, then Europe, in mere months. Ships, trains, planes, films, radio, television speed the spread of dance fashions.

Modern mambo, rumba and jive represent changing fashions in social dance, as did the *basse danse*, *pavane* and *galliard* centuries ago. Today, as in the past, dancing teachers help to alter tastes in dancing like designers in the world of dress. Partly through their influence, new dances rise, old ones disappear. Thus this century the Charleston, Big Apple, Lambeth Walk in turn gained fame, then died away. In recent years "old time" figure dances, needing skill and practice, have been revived.

Now, anyone can see the latest dancing fashion on his television set at home. Before his eyes professional dancers perform to perfection what is really just a social dance for the pleasure of the people who do it.

Inspired to imitate their dancing idols of film and television, people make up formation dancing groups. Ten or a dozen couples will perform a waltz, a tango or a foxtrot with perfect timing. No countermarching troops could keep formation better.

Teachers' associations, examining boards, international championships inspire formation dancers to ever greater efforts, ever greater skill. Seen from the television camera, high above, their interwoven movements remind us of some early ballet. Like the minuet before it, the social waltz has itself become a dance of entertainment rather than a social pleasure.

Little girl in Tokyo sees Russian ballet in American movie. Modern films and high-speed travel help to spread a dance around the world.

By imitating films that they have seen, people learn the social dances of most distant nations. At Chinese May Day celebrations men and women dance the European waltz in Peking's city streets.

Left: Medieval strolling entertainer performed with little more than juggler's cups and ball. Right: Artificial lighting and other scientific "props" enhance a modern dance performance.

Right: The "Can-Can" in 1900. Left: Modern dance. Changing fashions affect costumes but the movements of a dancer's body remain unaltered.

Living in a machine age we, more than our ancestors, feel the need to escape from the bustle of the mechanical world. Better paid than our ancestors, we can afford to step off the busy street and sink into the plush seat of a motion picture theatre. Ten years ago, over 230 million movie seats a week were sold throughout the world. Today, in the Western world, most families have their own television set.

Although some say we are the slaves of the machines we manipulate, we certainly make machines add to our enjoyment. Trick photography and cleverly designed film sets enable us to see such stars as Fred Astaire dance on tables, dustbins, battleships – dancing in situations the like of which we shall never see outside a film.

Films have helped to make classic ballet widely known. But the roving viewpoint of television cameras could perhaps help to create entertainment dances unlike either old ballets, seen only from above, or modern dancing, seen only from the side.

Thanks to modern science and machines, millions the world over can simultaneously see the world's greatest dancers on film. A century ago the biggest audience would have been a town's population gathered to see a rope dancer perform above their heads between the rooftops.

Rope dancers simply depended on a high wire slung across a street. Modern science helps to make dances still more spectacular. Created by modern freezing plant, artificial ice rinks attract audiences in the biggest cities in the hottest heat wave. On ice, formation dancing, figure skating, spectacular shows have given a new turn to entertainment dancing with jumps, turns, *pirouettes* and other steps borrowed from social dance and ballet. Freed from the limits set by gravity on dry land, a skater in an *attitude* can skim gracefully on one leg while "standing still."

But today, many people still patronize smaller, more intimate showplaces. They enjoy the atmosphere of music hall, theatre, cabaret, where actors and dancers can project their personality to an audience that they can see.

Although modern science and machinery produces trick filming, artificial ice rinks, even underwater ballet, the dancer still plays upon the same instrument as the acrobatic artists of ancient Greece and still more ancient Egypt – the human body.

No matter what new inventions of man's brain aid the spectacle of his dance, the movements of man's body remain the same as 20,000 years ago.

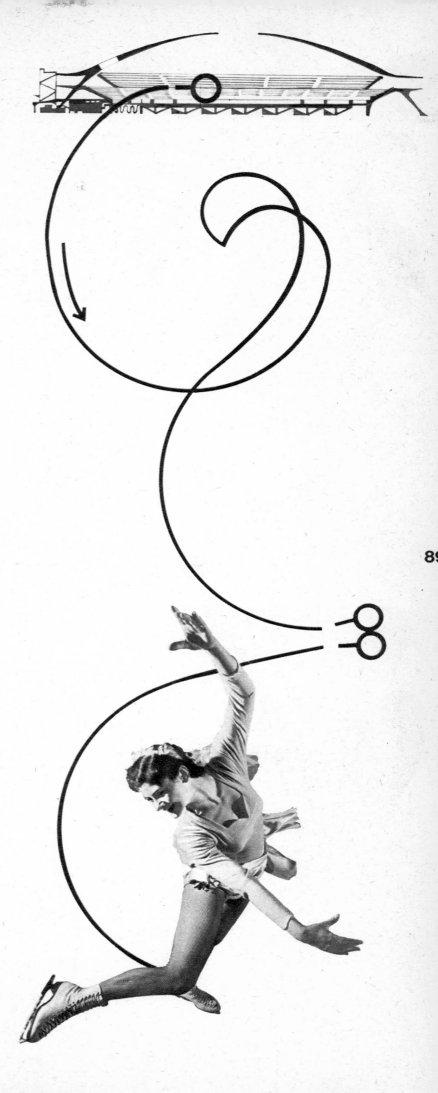

89

"West Side Story" reveals modern city life in music, drama, dance and scenery — combined as in the past in Athens and Versailles.

One modern sport stadium held nearly half a million spectators. Yet athletics, one of the greatest spectacles of our time, began life simply as a healthy exercise for the people who took part in it. So also dancing, once intended for the pleasure of peasant merrymakers, has become a city entertainment. Ancient folk dances still exist, but we know them better as spectators than performers when, at folk dance festivals, we see them on a stage.

Teams of expert folk dancers travel across the world, making better known the dance traditions of their homelands. But their fun and merrymaking, once spontaneous, must be acted – you cannot be naturally gay for seven performances a week.

The spontaneous dances still performed for pleasure in the experts' homelands are often different from the sights we see on stage. Experts, paid to dance, dress in brilliant national costumes. But peasant dancers often cannot afford new costumes when their old ones are worn out.

Today, dancing for enjoyment is becoming ever more enjoyed by those who watch and less by those who do it. People trying to escape from dancing as a regulated spectacle have helped to popularize the free-moving steps of modern rock 'n' roll. Yet even rock 'n' rollers imitate what they have seen on films.

We in the West no longer dance for magic. Yet the story of dancing is like a pendulum, swinging between magic and entertainment. We consider ourselves cultured to combine the arts of music, drama, painting, dancing in a modern dance-drama such as "West Side Story." We look back on Stone Age man's art as crude, feeble and forgotten.

But the magic dances of Stone Age man are not forgotten. They go on in the everyday lives of savage peoples in the world today. And some of us have learned to look on them for what they are – not childlike attempts to imitate ballet, but revealing a keen, instinctive understanding of rhythm – rhythm, without which no dance, not even life itself, could have its being. Even a ballerina can learn something from a dancing bushman.

Our survey shows that dancing does not age. Ceaselessly the dance renews itself. Persistent as the rhythms of the universe, it cannot be destroyed. Were our present civilization wiped out, the survivors would still dance in its ruins in fear, hope and worship. And from these spontaneous dances a new art of the dance would arise, and the cycle would start again as fields were tilled and cities rebuilt.

Dances of the age of Greece became forgotten. Yet magic dances, older far, remain. Were modern city life destroyed, dance as entertainment might die out but dance itself would never disappear.

Index

Credits

American Museum of Natural History 18 (above left), 21 (below); Anderson 43 (right); Antikensammlungen, Munich (Hirmer) 28 (below), 47 (above right); A.P.D.A.G.P. 59 (below); E. Louis Backman: Religious Dances (Allen & Unwin) 47 (left); Baron Studios 49 (above), 79 (above right), 81 (above); after Rudolph & Joan Benesh: An Introduction to Benesh Dance Notation (A. & C. Black Ltd.) 74 (above right), 75 (above); Bibliothèque Nationale 52, 61 (below left), 82 (left), 88 (above left); P. Black 22 (right); Black Star 7 (above right), 88 (above right); Franz Boas: Primitive Art (Sammenlignende Kulturforskning) 9 (above right); Anne Bolt 17 (above right) (below left), 45 (above), 88 (below left) (photo of Elizabeth Seal); Abbé Breuil 22 (above left); B.B.C. 23 (below right), 78 (upper middle), 79 (below right), 92; British Museum 14 (above left), 15 (below right), 24 (above), 42 (above left), 51 (left), 54 (right), 55 (left), 62 (above & middle), 63 (below); British Museum (Natural History) 8 (above); Bulgarian Press Bureau 11 (above right); Carrieri: La Danza in Italia (Editoriale Domus) 82 (right); J. Allan Cash 38 (below right); Jean Cocteau, from Richard Buckle: In Search of Diaghilev (Sidgwick & Jackson) 72 (left); Commonwealth Relations Office Library 12 (below), 41 (below); Conzett & Huber 18 (below), 44; Czechoslovak Travel Bureau 63 (above); Dance Notation Bureau Inc. 74-5 (below); Max Erlanger de Rosen 70 (all photos but lower two) 71 (below left); Raymond de Seynes 19 (above right); The Detroit Institute of Arts 13; English Folk Dance and Song Society (Biagoj Drnkov) 11 (above left); Fine Art Society Ltd. 26 (above right); Folkwangschule der Stadt, Essen 83 (below); Francis, Day & Hunter Ltd. 58 (left: above & below); French Tourist Office 45 (below), 64 (right); Gillsater-Reportage 23 (below left), 39 (below right), 47 (below); Giraudon 16, 25 (below), 60 (below), 68 (below), 71 (above left); Glasstone 28 (above right); Golden Head Press Ltd. 70 (above right); Graphische Sammlung Albertina, Vienna 46 (above); Rune Hassner 40 (below), 46 (middle), 58 (middle left & above right), 81 (middle), 86 (left), 87 (below); Heraklion Museum, Crete 28 (above left); Gerald Howson 4 (left), 7 (below), photos 34-8, 66-7 (below), 79 (left: above & below), 90; Michel Huet 59 (above); Don Hunstein 5 (right), 53 (middle), 85 (left); "Inforcongo," Brussels 12 (above), 20 (above), 91; Lincoln Kirstein 57; Kobun-Sha 87 (above); Boris Kochno: Le Ballet en France (Librairie Hachette) 61 (right) (Lipnitzky photo), 72 (right), 78 (above); Peter Larsen 10 (below), 56 (above left), 58 (below right); Dr. A. E. Laszlo 17 (left); Le Goubin 89 (below); Lelong 25 (above); Lipnitzky 73 (below); Angus McBean 78 (above); Ella Maillart 36 (left), 39 (above left); Mander-Mitchenson Collection 69 (middle); Mansell Collection 27 (below), 29 (below), 33 (left), 42 (above right), 51 (below), 53 (below right), 54 (left), 70 (below: left & right), 84 (right); Roger Mayne 8 (below), 15 (above right), 23 (above right), 86 (below right); M-G-M 80, 85 (right); Musée de l'Homme (Pierre Verger) 9 (below right); Musée des Arts Decoratifs 73 (above); Musée des Gobelins (J. E. Bulloz) 48 (above); Musée National des Arts et Traditions Populaires 14 (above right); Museo del Prado, Madrid (Manso Martin) 48-9 (above); Museo S. Marco, Florence 21 (above); Museo Nazionale, Naples (Parisio) 30 (below); National-bibliothek, Vienna 4 (right), 53 (above); National Publicity Studios, Wellington, N.Z. 19 (above left); Angelo Novi 30 (above); Lennart Olson 33 (right); Gerda Peterich 83 (above); Philbrook Art Center, Tulsa, Okl. 20 (below); Paul Popper 58 (middle right); Theodore Presser Co., Bryn Mawr, represented by Alfred A. Kalmus Ltd. 17 (music, left); Radio Times Hulton Picture Library 17 (below right), 51 (above right), 56 (below), 92; P.J.S. Richardson: Cecchetti photo 70; Rijksmuseum, Amsterdam 65 (above); Robbins Music Co. and Francis, Day & Hunter Ltd. 56 (above right); Houston Rogers 68 (above), 74 (above left), 78 (lower middle); Dr. H. Scharschuch 84 (left); F. Schlesinger 26 (below); Schuh 23 (above left); Shell photo 39 (below left); Smithsonian Institution 50 (below); S.C.R. 10 (above); Stiftsbibliothek, St. Gallen 27 (above); Tate Gallery 77 (right); Time Inc. 38 (above & below); Tokyo National Museum 39 (middle right); Victoria and Albert Museum 9 (below left) (R. L. Jarmain), 66 (above), 88 (below right); Vera Watkins 19 (below); Roger Wood 76 (above & below), 77 (left), 81 (below); photos passim by John Freeman; photos pages 4, 7, 66-7, 74, 79 of Anya Linden, ballerina of the Royal Ballet, Sadler's Wells; photos pages 36-8 of Sesha Palihakkara; Consultants: Maria Fay, Sesha Palihakkara.

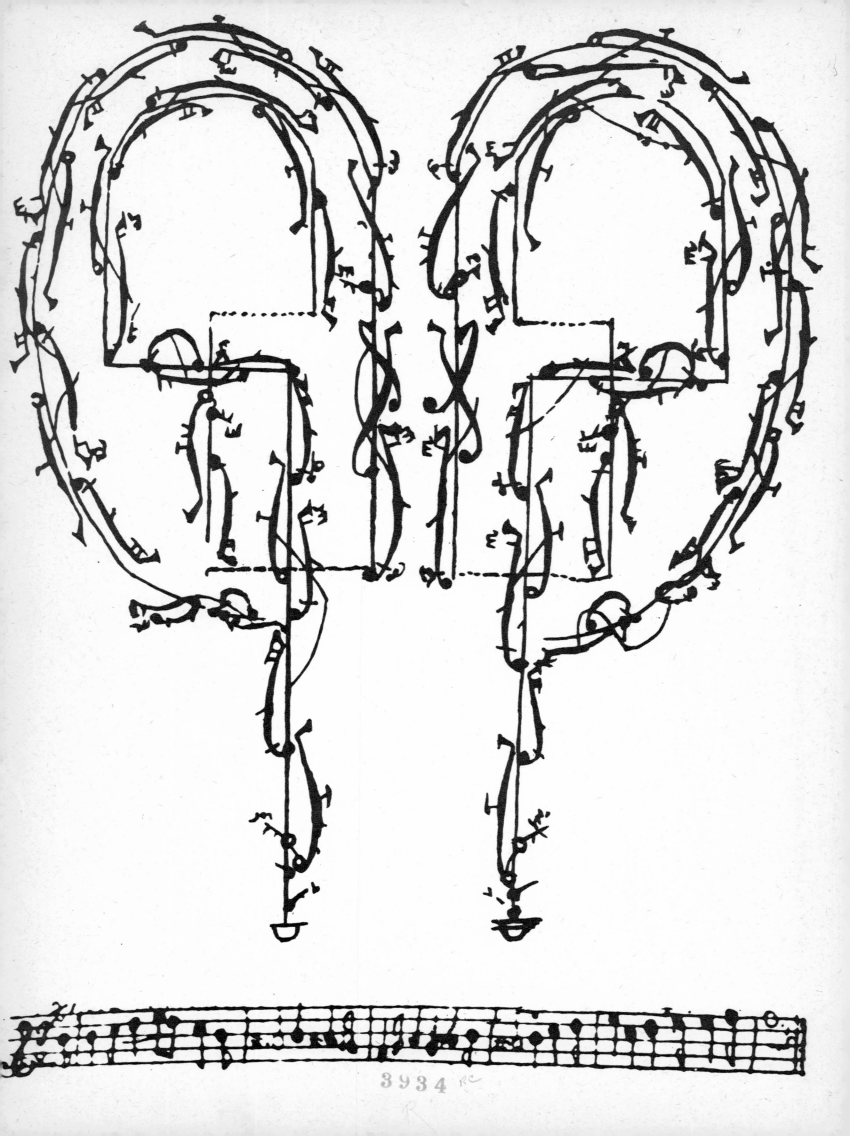